Music in West Africa

Music in West Africa

∞

EXPERIENCING MUSIC,
EXPRESSING CULTURE

∞

RUTH M. STONE

New York   Oxford
Oxford University Press
2005

Oxford University Press

Oxford   New York
Auckland   Bangkok   Buenos Aires   Cape Town   Chennai
Dar es Salaam   Delhi   Hong Kong   Istanbul   Karachi   Kolkata
Kuala Lumpur   Madrid   Melbourne   Mexico City   Mumbai
Nairobi   São Paulo   Shanghai   Taipei   Tokyo   Toronto

Published by Oxford University Press, Inc.
198 Madison Avenue, New York, New York, 10016
www.oup.com

Oxford is a registered trademark of Oxford University Press

Library of Congress Cataloging-in-Publication Data
Stone, Ruth M.
    Music in West Africa : experiencing music, expressing culture / Ruth M. Stone.
        p. cm. — (Global music series)
    Includes bibliographical references (p.) and index.
    ISBN 978-0-19-514500-7

    1. Music—Africa, West—History and criticism. I. Title. II. Series.

ML350.S76 2004
780'.966—dc22

                                                                2003070153

Printing number: 9 8 7

Printed in the United States of America
on acid-free paper

Contents

Foreword

∞

In the past three decades interest in music around the world has surged, as evidenced in the proliferation of courses at the college level, the burgeoning "world music" market in the recording business, and the extent to which musical performance is evoked as a lure in the international tourist industry. This heightened interest has encouraged an explosion in ethnomusicological research and publication, including the production of reference works and textbooks. The original model for the "world music" course—if this is Tuesday, this must be Japan—has grown old, as has the format of textbooks for it, either a series of articles in single multiauthored volumes that subscribe to the idea of "a survey" and have created a canon of cultures for study, or single-authored studies purporting to cover world musics or ethnomusicology. The time has come for a change.

This Global Music Series offers a new paradigm. Teachers can now design their own courses; choosing from a set of case study volumes, they can decide which and how many musics they will cover. The series also does something else; rather than uniformly taking a large region and giving superficial examples from several different countries within it, in some case studies authors have focused on a specific culture or a few countries within a larger region. Its length and approach permits each volume greater depth than the usual survey. Themes significant in each volume guide the choice of music that is discussed. The contemporary musical situation is the point of departure in all the volumes, with historical information and traditions covered as they elucidate the present. In addition, a set of unifying topics such as gender, globalization, and authenticity occur throughout the series. These are addressed in the framing volume, *Thinking Musically*, which sets the stage for the case studies by introducing ways to think about how people make music meaningful and useful in their lives and presenting basic musical concepts as they are practiced in musical systems around the world. A second framing volume, *Teaching Music Globally*, guides teachers in the use of *Thinking Musically* and the case studies.

The series subtitle, "Experiencing Music, Expressing Culture," also puts in the forefront the people who make music or in some other way experience it and also through it express shared culture. This resonance with global history studies, with their focus on processes and themes that permit cross-study, occasions the title of this Global Music Series.

Bonnie C. Wade
Patricia Shehan Campbell
General Editors

Preface

∽

I've been traveling to the Kpelle area of Liberia, West Africa since I was a young child, getting to know people, learning from them, and sharing their music, pains, and aspirations. I hope that this book will provide a glimpse of what I have been privileged to learn. This is a book about the music of West Africa. As I explain in the text, musical elements, principles, instruments, practices, and values are frequently held in common throughout West Africa. While I focus on the Kpelle musicians to explicate them, these elements apply to a much broader area of the West African area and should be understood in that light. There are some overarching themes that describe West African music in general and Kpelle music in particular: (1) Music is a tightly bound bundle that links sound to dance, instrument playing, and narration. (2) Performers in a broad range of musical events relate to one another in a part-counterpart arrangement where a soloist, for example, would have a supporting soloist. (3) The most valued form of performance is that in which short melodic and rhythmic patterns or motifs, performed by a variety of performers, are interlocked in a hocket arrangement.

I wrote this book in the Eastern Province of Saudi Arabia where I spent my summers while my husband worked. I brought copies of fieldnotes and texts in my suitcase as I traveled halfway around the world for my writing hiatus. As I poured over notes, happy memories of experiencing musical events with the performers flooded over me. At times, however, I was also overcome by sadness as I thought of the war that devastated Liberia shortly after I left in 1989 and the effects of the fighting that continue to ravage the country. Though a troubled peace has been brokered, many of the people with whom I worked are no longer in their homes and are living in refugee camps in Liberia or elsewhere in West Africa.

I recently heard from one of the musicians with whom I worked, Feme Neni-kole, and she is presently in the Buduburam Refugee Camp in Accra, Ghana. In a letter dated August 23, 2003, she wrote, "As normalcy is now returning to Liberia, we have formed an organization known as Association for Traditional Musicians in Africa (ATMA) so as to work with traditional musicians in Liberia and beyond"(Neni-kole 2003).

I am grateful to Rene Zabat who interpreted my handwriting from yellow pads and typed them into the computer. Susan Oehler, Clara Henderson, and Paul Schauert, my research assistants, provided a valuable reading and commentary on the text. I'm also indebted to Bonnie Wade and Patricia Campbell for their close interaction throughout this project, and to Bryan Burton for his work as a music education consultant. Finally, I owe so much to the musicians and research assistants in Liberia who patiently taught me what I have learned about Kpelle music. They are the experts who have shared their knowledge and their passion for performance. I only hope I have interpreted it for the readers in ways that they will recognize.

CD Track List

∞

1. "Ku Kelee Be Li" (We All Are Going). Christian song with indigenous themes, St. Peter's Lutheran Church Kpelle Choir, Monrovia, Liberia, 1989. Recorded by Ruth M. and Verlon L. Stone.
2. "Kalu Lee, Lee." Epic performance, Episode 5. Kpelle, Totota, Liberia. Performed by Kulung, 1976. This is the fifth episode from this particular rendition of the Woi-meni-pele, celebrating the deeds and adventures of the superhuman hero of the Kpelle people. Recorded by Ruth M. and Verlon L. Stone.
3. Transverse Horn Ensemble. Kpelle, Gbanga, Liberia. Performed by horn ensemble, 1970. These horn ensembles accompany chiefs when they travel to enhance their prestige. Recorded by Ruth M. and Verlon L. Stone.
4. "Sala Kpa Kpa." Kpelle, Totota, Liberia. Performed by a popular music group led by Moses and John Woni, 1976. These young men draw upon music from East Africa to inspire their transformation of Kpelle performance. Recorded by Ruth M. and Verlon L. Stone.
5. Bush Clearing. Kpelle, Yanekwele, Liberia. Performed by a work cooperative, 1976. These musicians encourage the workers who are cutting the forest to prepare the land for rice planting. This ensemble consists of five slit-drum players and singers. Recorded by Ruth M. and Verlon L. Stone.
6. Voice Disguise Using Drum Head, by master drummer, Kao Pee, 1976. Kpelle, Totota, Liberia. Recorded by Ruth M. and Verlon L. Stone.
7. "Giing." Kpelle, Totota, Liberia. Peformed by a group from Gbeyilataa, 1970. Two soloists, a female, Pona-woni, and a male, Wokpe, alternate their competitive lyrics with a chorus. They are supported by a goblet-shaped drum and a cylindrical drum. Recorded by Ruth M. and Verlon L. Stone.

8. Triangular Frame-zither. Kpelle, Totota. Performed by Flumo, 1976. The performer, combining overlapping multi-ostinato patterns creates visual images of a leopard hunting in the forest. Recorded by Ruth M. and Verlon L. Stone.

9. Musical Bow. Kpelle, Totota. Performed by Flumo, 1976. A hunting bow is held with one end resting on the performer's lap and the other with the mouth encircling the upper end of the string. The performer taps on the lower end of the string with his right hand and resonates the sound with his mouth at the upper end. Recorded by Ruth M. and Verlon L. Stone.

10. Women's Planting Song. Kpelle, Totota, 1976. Women work in a cooperative group to loosen the soil for planting rice. They work with short handled hoes, singing and advancing forward as they perform call and response songs. Recorded by Ruth M. and Verlon L. Stone.

11. Children's Counting Song. Kpelle, Totota, 1976. These children count in a call and response pattern. Recorded by Ruth M. and Verlon L. Stone.

12. Entertainment Love Song. Kpelle, Stuart's Farm (near Totota), 1976. Recorded by Ruth M. and Verlon L. Stone.

13. *Meni-pele* (Chante-Fable), Story-song. Kpelle, Sanoyea. Performed by Peter Giddings and ensemble, 1970. Recorded by Ruth M. and Verlon L. Stone.

14. Drum Pattern: *Kee kee zi-kee*, master drummer, Kao. Totota, 1976. Recorded by Ruth M. and Verlon L. Stone.

15. Woi Epic, Episode 2. Kpelle, Totota, Liberia. Performed by Kulung, 1976. This is the fifth episode from this particular rendition of the Woi-meni-pele, celebrating the deeds and adventures of the superhuman hero of the Kpelle people. Recorded by Ruth M. and Verlon L. Stone.

CHAPTER 1

Traveling to West Africa

∞

The time has come
Again
—*Taxi motto*

This book, centered on performance in West Africa, constitutes a conceptual journey. This journey will move through music—listening and analysis—to the western coast of West Africa. This region is an area of tropical rain forests, near the equator on the bulge of Africa, an area that has been known alternatively as the Guinea Coast, the Pepper Coast, and the Grain Coast. Some of the ideas encountered on this journey will seem far removed from what readers now know about music and performance in Africa. Other ideas will be warmly familiar. In response to these new concepts, you will need to identify your own approach so that you can understand what is significant to the people who create this music, what is most central to their way of thinking about music performance. The text will equip you to hear the music from the perspective of the people who create and experience it, even if you are unable to achieve that goal.

JOURNEYS

This journey parallels my own travels to Liberia, West Africa. I first went there to live at the age of three, and resided there until I was ready to enter high school (Figure 1.1). I became interested in learning about the music when I became an ethnomusicologist, a scholar who studies music as culture. On subsequent journeys over the last thirty years, I have documented the performance events of the Kpelle people who reside in Liberia and neighboring Guinea. This book is intended to take you to this place in order to experience some of the musical events that

1

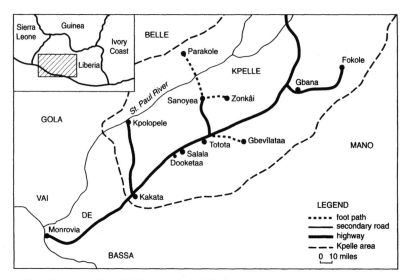

FIGURE 1.1 *Map of Liberia, West Africa.*

I have found—different, yes, but I hope you'll agree also—exquisite and moving.

As you move through this area, new landscapes and soundscapes will present themselves to you as they did to me: "The early morning ride from Monrovia was gorgeous, the mist down in the valleys encircling the hills. The smoke, rising from the kitchens, oozing from the thatch, the sun streaming through the rubber grooves" (Stone 1975:13). (Quotes cited "Stone 1975" are taken from my field journals, which I kept during my various trips to Liberia.)

In another scene, on a street in Monrovia, the capital of Liberia, a minibus stopped to pick up passengers at the side of the road. Reggae music played from the bus as it sped up from the stop. The assistant ran alongside the bus, and his steps appeared to be movement to the music.

Up the road from Monrovia, it was market day in Totota, some ninety miles inland. There, Kulung, an itinerant epic pourer was performing for a gathered audience, spinning his tales to the background of high-pitched percussion and the continuous chorus singing in the background. Laughter rippled through the audience, when a funny comment emerged in the story. The tales of Woi, the superhuman hero,

FIGURE 1.2 *Zawo Gotoko, my research assistant, 1975–76.* *(Photo by Verlon Stone.)*

centered on a journey too—one in which he was constantly running into obstacles.

In yet another scene, musicians negotiated with me and my research team for a recording session I had requested. Zawo Gotoko, my research assistant asked the musicians what they would like (Figure 1.2). The soloist deferred to an older man, for he explained, "Gaa ku polu," (He is behind us). Zawo commented, "We are all one, here," implying that we all shared the same aspirations for the recording session. Yaa, the older man, explained to the group that he had met me the day before yesterday. Then the singer asked for $15. Zawo and Yaa, the performers' representative, hung heads (conferred). They then brought me into the consultation. I offered $3. Zawo suggested I give $4, which would include $1 for the performers' liquor. I offered Yaa the money and he gave it to the musician, exhorting them to accept it (Stone 1975:15).

I was really glad to have someone assisting me like Zawo with his verbal skill, understanding the requirements of fieldwork, and having people of Kpelle descent acting in my behalf. This made it very much a Kpelle matter. Zawo was skilled at balancing the requirements of both sides and was able to offer a fair opinion on how much money the musicians should get. It was worth all the hassle I had to go through to keep him as my main research assistant. . . . The whole negotiation was incredibly interesting. It was treated most seriously. Rhetoric seemed important and in the end it was to the credit of Zawo and Yaa that they were able to impress their points through their status and their rhetoric (Stone 1975:18).

The journey in this book will include selected stops to pause to deeply reflect upon what you are hearing. You will be aware not only of what the music means to you as listeners, but what meanings are essential to different Kpelle people, members of an ethnic and linguistic group, who reside in Liberia and Guinea, West Africa. What lenses and earphones make up their toolkits when they hear these sounds? How might that awareness transform the way you listen to this music?

It's not easy to imagine how the Kpelle experience their music. But I'm going to attempt to provide some background to move you in that direction. I'll teach you about the meaning of such phrases as, "Ka ka woli too ndoo wuli ma, nke dooi, nke ma yorong bo," (Listen to my singing song, as I sing it, I open its net." When you've finished this book I hope you'll be able, at least to a degree, to contemplate what's important to some of the Kpelle people and how they regard performance. The Kpelle have a proverb, "A ke ba taa too, fêli-yale-nuu fe zu, ge ni taa fe," (If you build a town and there's no drummer in it, then it's not a town.) The proverb goes on to say, "If you build a town and there's no singer, then it's not a town." Such a saying hints at the central place music has in the lives of many of the Kpelle. For many Kpelle people, music performance is as much a part of a normal life as walking or talking or eating.

My first journey to West Africa, as I mentioned earlier, occurred in 1949 when I was a small child (Figure 1.3). At the age of three, my parents took my younger brother and me far from the midwestern United States where we had lived up to that time. We traveled by train to New York and then by propeller plane across the Atlantic Ocean. In those days the trip on Pan American Airways proceeded by stages. First, we flew to the Azores islands, which are located in the middle of the Atlantic, and then on to Lisbon, Portugal, where we stopped for a few days of sightseeing, provided by the airline. Then we flew down the coast of West Africa, stopping at Dakar, Senegal to take on passengers. Finally, we landed at Robertsfield, the international airport, located some forty miles from the capital of Monrovia. We subsequently drove

FIGURE 1.3 *Ruth Stone with family members in Liberia, c. 1955.*

over gravel roads to reach our home. Kpolopele was located some seventy miles from the coast in the gently rolling and thickly forested hills in the central Bong County area.

More recently I have made the journey by jet, flying from Indianapolis (near our home in Bloomington), to Chicago, London, and then down the coast to Robertsfield. My husband and I spent over a year in Liberia from 1975–76, conducting fieldwork for our doctoral dissertations (Figure 1.4). "It is quite amazing how the months in fieldwork pass. They seem to sometimes go past before you know that you have been working that month. Yet individual days can seem interminably long because there is so much packed into any one of them" (Stone 1975:206). I returned for several months in 1982–83 with my young

FIGURE 1.4   *Verlon Stone positioning video camera, 1975.*   *(Photo by Ruth M. Stone.)*

daughter and husband (Figure 1.5). In 1988, before the recent civil war broke out, I journeyed to Liberia on a Fulbright research grant in order to conduct field research, and a short time later my husband followed with our now eleven-year-old daughter, Angela Keema. After we arrived in Liberia, we drove a Volkswagon camper bus to move from one place to another. Much had changed about the journey since I had first traveled to Liberia some forty years earlier as a young child. We moved faster—jets had replaced propellers and computers had taken the place of manual typewriters.

Most importantly, during those forty years, I had moved great distances intellectually in understanding the music of the Kpelle perform-

FIGURE 1.5 *Angela Stone in Liberia, 1983. (Photo by Verlon Stone.)*

ers with whom I was working. As a young child I was home-schooled in Yanekwele, some ninety miles into the interior in Bong County, where we had moved from Kpolopele by the time I was ready for the first grade. My mother used the Calvert system for home-schooling, whereby at the end of every twenty lessons we sent tests to teachers in Baltimore for comment and evaluation. (During the time I grew up in Yanekwele, there was no English language school there.) The classroom time for American schooling lasted from about 7:00 to 10:30 a.m. each day. Then I was free to explore my Liberian "classroom" the rest of the day. During those hours I learned, without conscious effort, to speak Kpelle fluently. I also went to the rice fields with the local children, watching and helping as the women planted, weeded, and harvested the crop. I sat with them at their cooking fires as they spoke of the many parts of their lives. I went to the creeks and helped them fish with nets.

When I first returned to Liberia—as a student ethnomusicologist in 1970—I was a novice about the music. I began as a twenty-five-year-old researcher to listen, ask questions, and learn about why music mattered so much to many Kpelle people. As the blacksmith and ritual practitioner, Ge-weli-wula, said to me, "If you cry, then you must make music. Otherwise your heart will not be contented. If you are happy, you must perform. Otherwise your heart will not be contented." These words echoed in my mind as I attended a funeral with my research assistant, Zawo Gotoko, one day.

Zawo and I followed the procession at some distance. From the highway, Disayeei is a fifteen-minute walk through the rubber [planta-tion] and a swamp, then up a large hill. . . . The grave had been dug at the edge of town, adjacent to other graves. . . . The women stood off some distance from the grave and wailed loudly in pulsating sobs that began high in pitch and descended. Some shook. . . . Zawo and I returned to Totota at 5:30. The rest of the family walked past our place at dark (6:30). About 7:00 p.m. the musicians came with several family members, playing along the road and going into town.

After the musicians returned to town, they continued playing into the night. I still heard them at 11:00 p.m. They danced in a tight cir-cle, one woman carrying the lantern. The people did not even know that I was there (Stone 1975:25–26).

My trips as an ethnomusicologist were attempts to travel ever closer to the meanings about music that matter to the Kpelle musicians and audience members. I especially enjoyed the days when we walked to villages for interviews:

I took Martha and Zau, and we walked to Yilataa to interview Gbong-pilang and Saki Gating. It was a pleasant walk over. We had a de-lightful interview. The old men joked and the younger people gath-ered around as they told of the old history of the town. . . . At one point Gbong-pilang turned the interview around and began asking me questions about myself. He wanted to know if my husband had bought me. Ah well! . . . [On the way back] Zau talked about the things on the path. At the burial site that we had passed before, I no-ticed some cottonwoods growing. Zau remarked that it is the site of an old town. . . . It was raining, so Martha [held] the umbrella over the tape recorder. I got completely soaked to the skin. Reminded me of canoeing in the rain in Minnesota. But finally the rain let up and by the time we got to Massakoita, I had dried out (Stone 1975:281).

The way people share conversations, just as Zawo shared with me on the path, contributes to the partial sharing of values not only of culture in general, but of music in particular. The term culture describes such learned behaviors, and cultures differ because people living in disparate parts of the world, with a variety religious beliefs or family arrangements, or geographically separated communities tend to develop particular values for living. Within communities, individual people partially share those values, and individual life histories provide a certain aspect of uniqueness, even as they share some common aspects with the people they know best.

TOOLS

I work, first of all, by keeping a journal in which I record my thoughts, observations, questions, and schedule. The journal is a record of all kinds of data that will serve to jog my memory as I later try to recall what happened at a particular performance. Sometimes I write in complete sentences, other times I let fragments convey the thoughts that come to mind. Some of my entries are about the mundane aspects of everyday life. Here's part of my entry for April 1, 1976:

> This was also the day I went to get John Woni for an interview. When I showed up at his place, he asked if I had room for some things. . . . So John was packed and ready to leave. His bed was disassembled and we put the slats, headboard, footboard, and sides on the top carrier. Then he had a gunny sack of possessions, which we put in the car. Later he moaned that he had forgotten his gun. This seemed to be the sum total of his worldly possessions. We left his goods at the little settlement at the head of the Disayeei path. He is going to now leave them in Disayeei until he gets another job (Stone 1975:211).

While I write my journal for the most part in English, I conduct almost all my fieldwork in Kpelle, particularly the interviews. "I really live in a different world when I interview in Kpelle. (One of the people I interviewed insisted on speaking English. As he talked in English he transformed so many things to his concept of Western [ideas], and it is probably one of the worst interviews for that reason)" (Stone 1975:282).

(For this book, I asked my research assistant, Susan Oehler, to read those notes and mark the sections that she thought would be especially appropriate to include here. I then selected interviews to include from among her marked sections.) To supplement the written journal, my husband, Verlon, also took *still* and *video* photographs that provide many details of what has been said and performed. (Some of those photos are also included here to help you visualize the people and locations that are described.) Sound recordings support these visual images, and some of those sounds are contained on the accompanying compact disc to enable you hear the sounds of Kpelle performance.

While in Liberia quite a few hours of each working day were spent transcribing texts of interviews and songs. Over the years I worked with such assistants as Edward Goto, John Barclay, Yakpalo Dong, and Zawo Gotoko. We played the tapes, one section at a time, and wrote on yellow lined pads each phrase of text as we deciphered it. Only later did we translate the Kpelle into English, since that was a separate and distinct process. The transcripts and the translations of performance and interviews about music making were then further memory aids for work, such as this book, that would be written later about the field research.

I took lessons, and learned to play the *konîng,* the triangular frame-zither. Bena, the musician who made my instrument and then became my teacher, patiently helped me to learn the basic patterns and then to combine the left hand with the right hand part. He also shared the following knowledge that had not been disclosed in any earlier interviews I had conducted up to that time. "Bena explained to me that if I was learning, there should not be a lot of people around. This type of performance is considered private and, therefore, should not be taught in front of many people. Generally a fine player is thought to be the owner of a spirit, and this has engendered lots of funny discussion as to how I'm going to get one. If I play well, I'm sure I will be accused of possessing a [tutelary] spirit" (Stone 1975:263).

When I returned to the United States I then analyzed the meaning of all that I had experienced and felt during my "field research" in Liberia. My memory was jogged by the journal, still photographs, video recordings, transcripts, and translations. I was ready to recall, interpret, and recreate what I thought happened. I took into account the voices of the musicians and bystanders who shared their insights.

The raw data of many ethnomusicologists eventually is placed in archives where generations of future scholars and the interested public can study what they wrote and thought and what they recorded in the field. One of the largest and best known of the world music sound archives is the Library of Congress in Washington, D.C. (http://www. loc.gov). The speeches of presidents of our country and the texts of blues singers from the Mississippi Delta are preserved there as voices that have contributed to the cultural and historical record of the United States. Musical performances from all around the world are also housed at the Library of Congress. My own recordings and accompanying documentation have been placed in the Archives of Traditional Music at Indiana University, the largest university based sound archives in the United States (http://www.indiana.edu/~libarchm). If you visit the archive you can explore more comprehensive versions of what you read about in this book. One may even listen to the sound examples by visiting the facility on the campus in Bloomington, Indiana.

WEST AFRICA IN PERSPECTIVE

Many earlier travelers pre-dated my journey to West Africa. Abdullah Ibn Battuta, the inveterate Arab explorer, described his impressions of music performance in the ancient Kingdom of Mali, located to the northwest of Liberia in 1352 AD "In front of the Sultan go the singers holding gold and silver rattles; behind him are about three hundred armed slaves. The Sovereign walks leisurely. . . . Finally he slowly mounts the platform in the manner of a preacher mounting his pulpit: as soon as he is seated, they beat the drums, and sound the horn and trumpets" (Battuta 1858:406, 411).

Travelers, including missionaries and scholars, provided the earliest written accounts of music performance from Liberia. D. W. Whitehurst traveled to Bopolu in 1835 and described, among other things, the war drum: "The beating of the war drum is effected by the open hand, and requires great effort to accomplish it. The body of the drum resembles a mortar neatly fashioned, with places for the insertion of pieces of iron resembling a quiver, to which are attached rings of the same metal; the concession of the drum head gives them a tremulous motion, which by bringing them into contact with the upright produces a jingling noise" (1836:278).

Not until the journey of George Herzog in the early 1930s did an ethnomusicologist venture into the Guinea Coast area of Africa and make a detailed study of music performance. His recordings, made on the southeastern coast of Liberia were etched on wax cylinders, each recording lasting no longer than three minutes. The sounds on those cylinders are today preserved in the Archives of Traditional Music at Indiana University (Herzog 1930).

Travelers over the generations have learned that West Africa is a region where tropical vegetation increases in density as one moves inward from the coast. A broad band of thick forest then gradually gives way to savannah land as you travel even further inland, and the elevation increases. The tropical growth is fueled by rainfall of several hundred inches per year. Only on the northern fringe of West Africa is the Sahara Desert found.

The present-day residents of Liberia migrated from the 1500s to the 1800s from the grassland area down to the coastal area in the kingdom of Mali region—an area that encompasses the present country of Mali. As these peoples settled, they became slash-and-burn agriculturalists who raised rice as their main food crop. They also grew rubber, cocoa, and coffee as cash crops over the years.

While some people in West Africa have been and continue to be agriculturalists, many other people cluster in the urban cities of Freetown, Conakry, Monrovia, Lagos, Ouagadougou, Accra, and Abidjan. Highrise offices buildings, urban traffic, as well as television, computers, video clubs, and Internet cafes are part of the environment in the cities and some rural areas. Elementary and secondary schools as well as colleges, technical schools, and universities are found throughout the region. In Liberia, people from some sixteen ethnic areas speak their own language as well as languages of trade and commerce such as English, Mandingo, and French.

During the Middle Ages, several African kingdoms with large centralized governments emerged. In West Africa, the Kingdom of Ghana flourished in the grasslands area along the Niger River (700–1200 AD) followed by the Kingdom of Mali, which increased in size and influence (1200–1500). The Kingdom of Songhai (1350–1600) took the place of ancient Mali. There was also Benin, which flourished in the part of the present-day Nigeria from 1300–1800, as well as the Ashanti Kingdom in the location of contemporary Ghana (1700–1900). These ancient African empires engaged in long-distance trade of gold, ivory, and salt. With the accumulated wealth gained in trade, they retained large ensembles of royal musicians who were vital parts of state occasions.

These musicians served as agents of the rulers' power and through sound enhanced the kings' prestige in processions and performances. The sonic symbols amplified the visual symbols of power displayed in cloth, as well as gold leaf on swords, stools, and staves.

Visual images of some of these musicians are preserved in Benin bronze plaques that are today found in museums around the world. I was recently in the British Museum in London where there are several bronze plaques that show horn players as well as drummers from the Benin Kingdom.

Many of these ancient centralized states and their accompanying structures have evolved into forms that are largely symbolic, but exist in parallel to the national governments that rule from the capital cities. There are also much smaller scale political units, known as "stateless societies." These political formations may have several layers of chiefs who owe their allegiance to a national government. At the grassroots level, government is largely consensual. At the upper level, chiefs consult elders to make decisions. But these entities are much less hierarchical than the centralized kingdoms.

Part of this journey to West Africa will introduce you to social formations, which are characterized by extended families in which the residence may be matrilocal or patrilocal. That is, young people marry and reside either near the mother's or the father's family, and descent is reckoned through either the mother's or the father's line. As members of the family move to urban areas, and even to other countries, the ties persist even if new modes of interaction may be required. In many areas of West Africa, for example, urban dwellers regularly travel back to their home villages on weekends to attend funerals of deceased relatives. Thus, the extended family ties and patterns of relating persist to some degree even in cases where great distances separate members of the family.

In West Africa, the Poro and Sande (sometimes labeled "secret societies" by scholars) organizations are important social groups in certain areas. All adults in these communities are expected to become members and receive instruction in customs and values. Children leave their homes to live apart in Poro (for men) and Sande (for women) enclosures in the forest.

Part of the education acquired is musical. Young adults emerge at the end of their educational session and demonstrate the dances they have learned as part of their preparation for adulthood. An essential aspect of the graduation exercise is a display of the dances that everyone has learned to perform. For the very talented young people there is specialized training beyond the Poro or Sande for becoming vocal, instrumental, or dance soloists.

When traveling throughout West Africa, you will notice that there is great variety in religious beliefs and practices. In the indigenous practice, a high creator god rules. People contact the intermediate deities through divination—spiritual attempts to predict the future and prescribe solution—worship and sacrifice. And these intermediate deities, who inhabit water, plants, and rocks serve as intermediaries to the high god. The Kpelle people variously adhere to indigenous religion, Christianity, and Islam as well as other religions, sometimes drawing on several at one time. There are also some Christian churches that integrate aspects from several of these other religious systems.

Though some colonial accounts have portrayed Africa as a "sleeping" continent awaiting the arrival of Europeans, trade and travel long predates the coming of the Portuguese in the 1500s and the other Europeans who followed. There is good evidence that enterprising Southeast Asians brought crops such as rice. The Arabs traveled back and forth across Africa nearly five hundred years before the Europeans arrived for the first time. Thus, there is reason to suggest that there was extensive travel, and subsequently, trade across Africa for hundreds of years before the first Westerners arrived.

The arrival of the Europeans brought with it the colonization of the many areas within Africa, and the subsequent influences of each particular European country upon its particular colony. Thus Ghana and Nigeria, for example, have considerable British influence in social and cultural matters and are known as Anglophone countries. On the other hand, Senegal and Mali, are known as Francophone countries because of the French influence brought to them while they were colonies of France.

Liberia was never a colony of any European country. Nevertheless, it was influenced by the United States because African Americans were repatriated to Liberia by the American Colonization Society beginning before the American Civil War. These "settlers" became a powerful national group and dominated the national government until the civil war in 1989. A variety of American and European missionaries also came to proselytize people. One result of these various contacts is that many Liberians use American first names or surnames though others have reverted to their indigenous names.

As a traveler to West Africa you might notice the old forts along the West African coast and wonder about their history. These were places where Africans were held before being shipped to the New World as slaves. These forts played a part in the tragic aspects of West Africa's history when families and villages were split apart and humans were treated most inhumanely. Some of the travelers to Africa today are the descendants of those slaves who are coming back to visit and learn of their ancestral home.

Trade routes crisscrossed West Africa from the days of the Arabs, and people traveled on foot or on animals. Modern highways throughout West Africa from around the 1950s greatly increased the pace of movement. Fresh produce could be quickly shuttled from interior villages to urban markets. Taxis and buses enabled people to travel from interior homes to urban work places and back again at month's end. With all of the movement, music cassettes of the latest popular world music have long been available for purchase. West Africans listen to James Brown, Bob Marley's reggae, or rap at various times. They see videos of the latest movies whether from the South Asian, East Asian, or Hollywood film industries. They listen to local, regional, national, and continental musical artists. Or they may play the British Broadcasting Company's classical music as I heard in the Totota welding shop next to our house.

MUSIC IN THE ARTS AND LIFE

Music and dance are so closely bound together in the thinking of many West Africans that it is difficult to separate song from movement or playing the drum from speech. Even drama is part of this tightly bound complex of the arts. The Kpelle people of Liberia, for example, use the term "sang" to describe a beautifully executed dance step, a well-sung song, or an elegant drum pattern. These various media blend one into another as when a drummer might say of a dancer, "The dance she spoke."

It is, in fact, difficult to find a word in any of the West African languages that is equivalent to the Western idea of "music." Instead there are terms for more specific actions like singing, drumming, or dancing as well as broader terms such as performance, which encompass song as well as dance, oration as well as instrumental playing. The isolation of music as sound is quite foreign in the conceptualization of most West Africans.

> The ideal in performance appears to be multiplication of things. . . . Yet when one considers the singing of a proverb, one apparently has the opposite, a rich concentrated statement put concisely without repetition. . . . [The Kpelle] say things like, 'There are many meanings to that'. . . . But part of the pleasure of proverbs is that they represent a . . . variety of connections to be made. And people find that delightful (Stone 1975:357).

The arts are also closely tied to the fabric of everyday social and political life. Music in the form of highlife songs in Ghana has promoted candidates for national office; music in the form of sung poetry has helped bring down a political regime and change the course of history in Somalia. Performance in many countries in West Africa has helped to develop AIDs prevention awareness.

Life cycle events such as birth, puberty initiation, and death are marked by musical performance. In all of these arenas, the arts are central to the flow of life. At a celebration for the birth of a child in Felela, Liberia,

> A group of 15–20 people congregated in an open spot near the house where the baby had been born. There were two instrumentalists playing buckets. One served as a *fêli* [goblet drum] player and the other served as a *gbung-gbung* [two-headed supporting drum] player. A young woman sat near the instrumentalists and was the soloist. Other women, however, took over the solo line occasionally. The songs were entertainment songs infused with lines pertinent to the present event. Both men and women took turns dancing in the center (Stone 1975:21).

On another occasion, we walked into the village of Disayeei as the relatives gathered for the wake of a taxi driver.

> Zawo asked me for 25 cents in small change which he would use to negotiate my attendance at the wake. He approached the person sitting in the center of the semicircle of men and gave him ten cents, saying that I (Kiape) 'gbulong dia a nei' tie myself to them with ten cents. Then the people discussed whether I could stay. The town chief, Joseph Tinge, explained to the group who I was, who my father was, and that we had brought letters from various government officials saying that we were to be allowed to observe events. The matter 'reached' various people (Stone 1975:23).

They agreed that I could stay and attend the wake.

> Then Zawo gave them fifteen cents, explaining that "Kiape has made the death with fifteen cents" (Kiape aa zaai ke a ee-ti). As we sat there, other people brought money. One man acting like a master of ceremonies would take the money and give it to the other person overseeing the proceedings, repeating what the person had said. Then before the money was accepted, the relationship and obligations were discussed. In giving the money, the expression heard was, "Tuma ka ti kwa bu zaai mei" (Here are the leaves we are putting on the corpse) (Stone 1975:23).

A drum ensemble played continuously during the wake. By being with people and experiencing their lives and their music, I began to slowly understand how music intertwined in so many dimensions of Kpelle life.

The idioms, which are known in the West as "folk," "popular," "religious," and "art" are closely bound together for the most part in West Africa. This is the case for Djimo Kouyate, who plays the twenty-one stringed harp-lute (Kora) of Senegal, performing a fusion of indigenous music and world beat (Brown 1994). In another case, Baaba Maal recorded his album, *Firin' in Fouta*, in three phases, each reflecting a different kind of music. He began by returning to his ancestral village in Podor, which is in northern Senegal. There he recorded local, indigenous performance. Next, he moved to Dakar where he and his band transformed these sounds into rhythm tracks in a studio. Finally, he took the tracks to England where, in another studio, he added Celtic instruments, synthesizer sounds, and vocal tracks. Thus, local West African music blended with high-tech Euro-American popular music (Himes 1995 as quoted in Stone 1998:8).

In the Liberian Lutheran church, Kpelle musicians have drawn upon indigenous themes and motifs associated with the Poro and Sande organizations to create meaningful expressions for their Christian worship. Musical motifs and singing styles have been layered into Christian worship practices. Texts, for example, compare Jesus to a ritual priest in the Poro. (CD track 1).

ACTIVITY 1.1   *CD track 1: Ku Kelee Be Li (We All Are Going), St. Peter's Lutheran Church Kpelle Choir, Feme Nenikole, soloist (3:38)*
This song alludes to the power of Jesus, referring to him as the big, big ritual priest in the Poro. The song also alludes to the mortality of all people, indicating that all will die as the text indicate, "We all are going." This provides a veiled political protest against Samuel Doe who was the military ruler of Liberia when this song was recorded. The singing style and instrumental accompaniment draws inspiration from performance for Poro and Sande ritual performances.

1. *Identify each time the soloist sings and then each time the chorus responds.*
2. *Clap to any part that you wish and keep with the ensemble as it performs. Are the claps equally or unequally spaced?*

In a similar way, in Kwabena Nketia's composition from Ghana, *Volta Fantasy*, both Western and African elements are prominent (Euba 1992:308).

STYLE AREAS

West Africa, as a region of Africa, is well-known, particularly within its indigenous music, for polyrhythmic, multilayered sounds. These fascinating constructions will serve as the focus of this book as you attempt to understand how such style characteristics relate to and influence the other arts and broader aspects of culture.

Just as interesting within West Africa, however, are the influences from North Africa and the Arab world that have been introduced by the traders over the centuries. This contrasting emphasis, in North African music, on more single-layered sounds as opposed to the multilayers that are so characteristic of West Africa, appears to have penetrated into many aspects of West African performance. Travelers have carried these ideas into West African communities over the centuries.

IDEAS ABOUT PERFORMANCE

There are some basic concepts that frame the way Kpelle performers and audience members think about the performances they experience. One of these concepts is the idea that performing in West Africa is like speaking one's native language. Everyone is expected to be able to sing and dance to a certain level of competence. Beyond that, talented young men and women are selected for special training. In other cases, families of musicians train children born into the lineage to carry on their parents' occupation. This is particularly true for the praise-singing *griot* or *jeli* of West Africa (Charry 2000:109).

Truly excellent performers rely, in many cases, upon the aid of supernatural tutelary spirits who are guides and spiritual teachers. Musicians may call upon these spirits to be present at a performance, though they refrain from talking openly about these relationships. These spirits form an elusive audience at the event and their presence may be known to only a select few of the human participants. They can also exact high demands from a singer for helping to enhance their performance. These demands can make a famous soloist's life difficult, sometimes even costing them their lives. Thus, beliefs about the religious and spiritual world are bound into the fabric of performing.

MUSICAL INSTRUMENTS

As you move from country to country, you'll notice that the musicians of West Africa play a rich array of indigenous and imported musical instruments. Beyond the expected variety of drums, they play the harp-lute (*kora*), lutes, zithers, rattles, plucked llamellophones, and struck instruments of many forms. Drums can be hourglass, goblet-shaped, conical, or cylindrical. They may be single headed or double headed and played with hands or sticks. Electric guitars and synthesizers are becoming ever more part of musical ensembles. West African musicians and other musicians of the world have adapted these instruments for their use, just as musicians performing African-American music have drawn on indigenous African instruments for their performance.

Instruments in this area are more than material objects. Rather, they often are considered quasi-human as they take on human features. These instruments, usually played by master musicians, may be given personal names, kept in special houses and "fed" sacrificial food. A drum that I encountered was called Goma by the musicians, a name given to a woman and meaning "share with me." They pointed out the ears, body, waist, and feet, all human features attached to the carved form. And when I finished field work with the ensemble that played Goma, the musicians sent her home with me as a gift (Figure 1.6). So now I bring "her" to class at Indiana University to show my students her features and let them play her to obtain a feel for creating sound on this well-used and played instrument. This drum with a woman's name reminded me of B. B. King, a well-known blues guitarist who has called his guitar by a woman's name also—in his case, Lucille.

Ethnomusicologists employ the Sachs-Hornbostel classification of instruments. In this system, they designate instruments as membranophones (where sound originates from a stretched membrane), chordophones (where sound originates from a stretched string), aerophones (where sound originates from vibrating air) and idiophones (where sound originates from vibration of the material of an instrument that has not been altered, through stretching, for example). Within West Africa, there are multiple examples within each category.

The peoples of West Africa have their own classifications of instruments. The Kpelle people of Liberia, for example, have two, rather than four, categories for their own instruments. All instruments are either blown (*fee*) or struck (*yale*). The first category coincides with aerophones in the Sachs-Hornbostel system and the second with all the other Sachs-Hornbostel categories. This local classification works because all

FIGURE 1.6   *Goblet-shaped drum, Fêli.*   *(Drawing from photo by Verlon Stone.)*

Kpelle stringed instruments are plucked, rather than bowed, and the finger, in their view strikes the string (Stone 1982:55–57). Other cultures emphasize male or female attributes of instruments, and many label individual strings of instruments with social designations such as chief, father, mother, or child.

CONCLUSION

West African music exists in a region of the world where many languages are spoken by different ethnic groups of people. There are a number of different national governments with varied economies. My own particular experience as a young girl and later as an ethnomusicologist has been predominantly in a village setting among Kpelle performers. The case study presented here primarily incorporates performance from the rural area, including influences, nevertheless, from the urban life.

If you were to examine the whole continent of Africa, you would find even more variation among the assorted cultures and nations. African musics, though quite different individually, share common cultural characteristics. African-American music, in addition, shares certain style characteristics with West African music, in particular. Descendants of West African and Central African people, who were enslaved by American and European colonial powers from the 1600s to the mid-1800s, brought their musical values with them and practiced that music despite the forced departure from their homelands and the inhumane conditions enforced by slave traders and owners. The travels of people from America to Africa and the other direction, as well, have contributed to the music that we are studying on this journey.

CHAPTER 2

Performance Facets

∞

This journey in search of music in West Africa up to this point has focused on the general surroundings that relate to music performance. The perspective so far might be called a bird's-eye view of the area. With that broad view established, the focus is about to shift to what might be termed a jeweler's-eye-view of performance. If you were examining a gemstone, it would be viewed with a jeweler's loop that contains a magnifying glass. This perspective shows details of the jewel and this jeweler's-eye-view, by analogy, will show us the rich facets of performance. These small parts within a performance will also be referred to as facets throughout this book.

The journey that was begun in the first chapter stopped in Totota, Liberia, about ninety miles from Monrovia. It was market day, a Wednesday, and the crowds had gathered from the nearby forest towns to sell some produce, buy a piece of cloth, or farm tool, or to just visit with friends. Yasie Brown sold cassette tapes along with many other items in his booth (Figure 2.1). "Cloth with picture of [President] Tolbert for sale. His name is printed beneath. . . . Cigarette seller calling to people, 'Ci-gar-rette-o.' Cloth seller ringing a school bell. . . . Other sellers call 'Ka pa ku poni too, oh' " [Come let's make market, oh] (Stone 1975:12).

In a backyard, not too distant from the market street, Kulung, an epic singer was preparing to begin his performance of the Woi epic, a story that is familiar to Kpelle people because in earlier years it was routinely performed in Gbeyilataa and other village communities around Liberia. A soft mat had been placed on the ground, and he knelt there as he made sure that his supporting performers were in place (Figure 2.2). The people from Gbeyilataa, some eight miles from Totota, formed the bulk of the crowd. One man agreed to be the questioner, while two young men began to tap the bottles to form the interlocking background

FIGURE 2.1   *Totota market.*   *(Photo by Verlon Stone.)*

rhythm for the performance. Four more young men and women from the assemblage sat together on a bench where they formed the chorus that, together with the instrumentalists, created the backdrop for the epic performance (CD track 2).

ACTIVITY 2.1   *CD track 2: Kalu Lee, Lee (Bowl Mother, Mother) Woi Epic performance, Episode 5 (4:30)   Kpelle, Totota, Liberia. Performed by Kulung, 1976.*
Two struck bottles provide the instrumental background. This is the fifth episode from this particular rendition of the Woi-meni-pele, celebrating the deeds and adventures of the superhuman hero of the Kpelle people.

1. *Identify the order of the staggered entries of the soloist, chorus, and struck bottles. Who or what comes in first? What follows*

FIGURE 2.2 *Kulung, Epic pourer.* *(Photo by Verlon Stone.)*

next? What enters last? These different parts—voices and instruments—with their contrasting timbres form aspects of the facets of performance.

2. *Describe the way the voices and instruments interrelate once everyone is performing. What changes take place as the performance proceeds. How, for example, does the performance of the storyteller-soloist change?*

VOCAL FACETS IN EPIC PERFORMANCE

Woi-meni-pele is a genre of Kpelle performance that centers on the hero Woi. Woi is a man constantly on the move, a superhuman ritual specialist, a Kpelle person first among all other Kpelle. As he moves himself and his family, he inevitably meets obstacles. On one occasion, Woi's house, which is moving, meets an anthill. To pass the anthill, Woi enlists the aid of an anteater and a mole who work in tandem to dig the earth and make a tunnel beneath the ground in order that the house might find a path to pass under the anthill (Stone 1988:11).

> About noon, one of the . . . little boys from Yilataa walked into the house with a man. . . . The boy explained that he knew the man told epic in Yilataa and so had brought him to me. The man, Kulung, was a rather gregarious . . . man who had obviously never been recorded, knew nothing about these matters, and was anxious to perform. He said that the Yiltaaa people would form the chorus. (Stone 1975:196).

And so it was, one of the most important musicians whom I recorded was brought to my attention by a young child who had watched my research and knew what I was studying. Epic pourers were at that time rare in the Kpelle area of Liberia. The demand for their live performances in the evening was being replaced by recorded audio and video recordings. "[Kulung-bai-miling-koli] now lived in a small town near Koloboi bearing his name. . . . His father came from Borola, south on the main road" (Stone 1975:197).

As Kulung started performing, he demonstrated first the chorus part before he launched into his own song and narration. Like a Southeast Asian *dalang* (puppeteer), he conducted the entire event, alternating between his part and other parts. He also narrated, sang, and dramatized the story by turns. Meanwhile, in the background the short, ever-repeating patterns of the bottles and the chorus members interlocked, all creating a kind of warp for the epic-pourer, Kulung to use as he wove his sound.

The musical backdrop, a multi-ostinato, served as an endlessly repetitive frame and the foundation to which Kulung joined his unfolding narrative stream. This multi-ostinato could be considered comparable to the drone in South Asian music or the clave in a Latin American dance song. What made all of this so fascinating were the facets that were displayed in the course of creating this very long epic, which was viewed as a story without end. The Kpelle creators deliberately broke the longer performance into smaller bits and pieces before combining them into a whole. As an audience member described the process:

> He would just go halfway and then jump on another. Halfway and jump on another. . . . But this woi-meni-pele is just going on and on, without any end. Woi is the person who is always present (Stone 1975:292). The teller himself expresses the ideal of perpetual motion when he says, "A ke no pong-pong ni (It was just [the sound of something in motion like monkeys in the bush moving from tree to tree])" (Stone 1975:203).

While listening to the chorus part, it is clear that there were really two different groups singing the chorus (CD track 2). The first began: *Kalu lee, lee* (Bowl, mother, mother); then the other group responded: *Kalu lee lee* (Bowl, mother, mother), using different pitches to distinguish their parts. Thus, what could easily have been an extended choral phrase was divided and faceted between two groups who alternated singers for the episode. This had been done for the aesthetic pleasure that the performers derived from such faceting. The texts of the choral parts were integrally tied to the story of the episode where Woi's jealous wife had been banished to the fork of the road to carve bowls with her magical voice. The chorus referred to her as the creator or "mother" of the bowls.

In the same way, the instrumental part might have been constructed so that one player executed the whole rhythmic pattern. Instead, the two players interlocked and alternated, together creating the resulting rhythm.

Each episode of the more than fifteen episodes performed that day had its own choral response, and the musicians shifted to the new patterns as the "pourer" moved to the next episode. In one episode the two choral parts were much more contrastive in text than the first example: *Ka doli e pa-o* (Call him to come, oh), with the second part singing: *Ziang kpono* (Ziang in person).

Another kind of faceting of the epic took place as the questioner asked his formulaic "Whose song is that?" With that prompting, the pourer began the narrative section. The questioner punctuated the flow of performance as it came from the pourer and the assembled musicians.

In yet another kind of faceting, at the end of an episode, the pourer said, "Dried millet breaking, *wese*" [sound of breaking] and the chorus responded, "*wese*." Thus, they jointly constructed the facet that terminated the episode, making room for a transition to the next episode. The onomatapoeic sound, *wese*, as a symbolic breaking of millet showed that sound was now being imitated as the episode ended (see Chapter 3 for a more detailed discussion). Action symbolized by sound in one area paralleled action in another. Most predominant here was vocal faceting where the voice broke sound into small sections and then combined them into a complex synchrony.

Kulung as an epic pourer was one of those very experienced and accomplished performers.

It seems that one is better off seeking musicians who can be reflective and explicit as much as possible. This appears to me to be the older and more renowned musicians. . . . For instance, the young singer, Kpana, was very well able to give us the text that he had sung. He seemed competent in constructing his song. But he saw no meaning in his music for people. He was not interested in what implications there might be in what he said. In fact, he kept saying, "Wulei woo no ka ti" (That's just song words) (Stone 1975:58).

The people from Gbeyilataa appeared to help with text transcription. We had nearly twenty-five people here most of the morning. That many people is really too many to transcribe a text. People all talk and argue, and it is difficult to find out what the text is that the first person tried to tell me. Sometimes, though, I should record one of these sessions. There are lots of very important comments made at these sessions (Stone 1975:59).

INSTRUMENTAL FACETS IN A HORN ENSEMBLE

Chiefs in Kpelle country, particularly important ones, move from place to place with royal musicians. These days, rulers enhance their prestige by ordering musicians from the countryside to come and play for state occasions. Master drummer, Kao, explained to me, "Our old president who was over us, President Tubman, his playing that was done, if you didn't have a master drummer in your town, you paid a $50–60 fine if you couldn't take a group to the place" (1975:63).

The next stop on the journey was a few miles farther north, forty miles or so, at Gbanga the administrative capital of Bong Country. There was a celebration for a visiting dignitary, and one of the neighboring chief's horn ensembles was playing (CD track 3).

C

ACTIVITY 2.2 *CD track 3: Transverse Horn Ensemble, Gbanga, Liberia (1:02)*

1. *Identify the various instrumental sounds that are being played. In what way is the ensemble similar to and different from the epic performance in CD track 2?*
2. *Clap one of the rhythms that you can feel as the ensemble plays.*

In this instance, the musicians were dressed in tunics and head-dresses that had pieces of leopard skin sewn into them (Figure 2.3). Red cloth trimmed the outfits. Four of the musicians were playing transverse carved ivory horns, rare instruments these days. They played the horns like one would blow a trumpet, changing their vibrating lips to alter the pitches that they played. A supporting drummer struck several goblet drums, fastened together into an assemblage known as *bala* (sheep).

Each of the four horn players was playing a very short motif—only one or two notes long that he interlocked with the other short motives of his fellow player. Because the music moved rather quickly, the horn players had to play very precise rhythms so that their short facets combined appropriately into the pattern that resulted.

The individual pattern could be thought of as an *ostinato* or repeated motif. All of the patterns together were combined to create a multi-ostinato that ultimately became the larger whole of the music composition.

Another term for combining short motives into a larger pattern is *hocket*. And this piece performed by the horns is a fine example of *hocketing*.

ACTIVITY 2.3 *Hocketing by Horn Ensemble*
You might want to look at how a different horn ensemble is doing just what has been described using a graphic notation. On the CD-ROM Music and Culture of West Africa (Gibson and Reed 2002), you can see visually as well as hear how the

FIGURE 2.3 *Horn player with leopard skin costume.*   *(Photo by Verlon Stone.)*

different parts play. You can even try playing one of the horn parts on your computer keyboard. And finally, you can compose your own horn ensemble music and listen to it played back.

As I talked to Kpelle musicians about what kinds of performance they most valued, they told me that the highest form of performance, from their viewpoint, was when musicians combined these facets or short sound facets to create the synchronized whole. Such faceting was considered to be quite wonderful and much to be valued over everyone singing or playing in unison—that is, performing the same music together at the same time.

It's fascinating that as a ruler, such as a chief, appeared at an official function, his (there are a few women chiefs) bearing and presence were enhanced by the sounds that were played. A few chiefs had horn ensembles using carved ivory instruments, but more commonplace were the horns carved from a lightweight wood used by most of the ensembles.

The audience that observed this spectacle had come to value the horn players who created a composition that required split-second timing and how the ensemble symbolized the ultimate in cooperation between multiple players. The most valued form of music was attached to the political leader who used these sounds to reinforce his status.

One of the keys to Kpelle music making rested within the two highly valued performance traditions just sampled. Faceting was important to the Woi epic. About this foundational oral narrative, the Kpelle say, "If one knows Woi epic, one knows Kpelle life" (Stone 1988:1). Faceting was equally valued in the music associated with the political rulers. Both of these high-status performance genres employed this valued technique.

Is this faceting an important feature in all Kpelle music? The answer is that while there are many examples in which one can detect faceting, one can also find music with somewhat different features.

CONTINUITY IN PERFORMANCE: WONI ENSEMBLE

The next stop, moving back toward the coast, was down the major highway that bisects Liberia. Traveling past Totota where Kulung performed, the pause in the journey came just past Salala, a fairly large town. Just south of it was a small hamlet inhabited mainly by workers in the nearby rubber plantations. In fact, the rubber trees began at the edge of the houses and the cups to catch the dripping latex were attached to each mature tree.

I greeted two young men who were rising stars of local popular Kpelle music in the mid 1970s. They created music by drawing from sounds of other African countries. Moses Woni, the lead singer who at that time wore an Afro haircut and bell-bottom trousers, headed the ensemble (Figure 2.4). His companion, lead drummer John Woni, was

FIGURE 2.4   *Moses Woni and John Woni, performers.*   *(Photo by Verlon Stone.)*

complemented by a changing supporting cast of chorus members, depending on who was in town at any moment. What I heard were long, continuous phrases that were quite the opposite of the short facets of the epic or the horn ensemble.

As Moses recounted the history of the group:

> When John was in school here, I was in Maimu and I didn't know him at that time. I first knew him from his soccer playing. He was a soccer player and was famous. We came to watch his soccer playing. I knew him but he didn't know me until I started singing. So he heard me sing and wanted to see me. Right now people want to see me but they don't know me. When we go to towns that we haven't been to

before, the people throng there, and there isn't even a place for us to stand next to each other. That's how it was that he came to know me and I came to know him.

I began this singing in 1972. I did it alone, with the people from my home. In 1973 I started singing in Totota. . . . I played for two years, and during the third I met John. I played the goblet drum and sang. . . . When we started playing together, I played the gbung-gbung (Stone 1975:149).

John Woni continued the history:

The way he was playing it, it was something new to our eyes. So one day I said to him, teach me to play the gbung-gbung [two-headed cylindrical drum] like you play it. Having taught me, he now plays the fêli [goblet-shaped drum]. We've showed all the people at the farm and they can't do it. That's why if we're playing we can't stand and dance. . . . We went to the camp where we lived in August 1974. . . . We haven't put the guitar in our performance. We are still learning it. I'm the one who can play it a little. When I learn well, I will teach him (Stone 1975:150).

It was the end of the month, their fellow rubber camp residents had been paid, and everyone was settling in for an evening of celebration.

When we arrived in the early evening, Moses Woni and the group were seated on the bench under the big tree by their house, playing with a crowd of younger children around them. When we came they were working with the guitar in the ensemble. They put it away when we got out of the car and went into their house to dress. When they came out, as we were setting up, they really seemed aware of the technology, interested and trying to wait until we set up before playing anymore, even though they had been playing when we arrived. . . . Performers sat for the first song in very close proximity, usually touching one another. The chorus clustered about the main performers and the audience about them. Later, when they stood up to perform and dance, there was a closed circle with the main performers at the nucleus (Stone 1975:103).

Moses Woni started by introducing himself to the audience, and the other lead performers followed suit, something that no soloist in other Kpelle performance had done in my experience. He then began spinning out the text of the first song that he and John had created together and one that was very popular with the young people. As John said in an interview, " . . . no matter where we go, if we sing the other songs they will ask us to sing 'Sang nong' (Stone 1975:197). The song described the adventure and mishaps of love relationships (CD track 4).

ACTIVITY 2.4   CD track 4: Sala Kpa Kpa (The Big, Big Sacrifice), Woni Group, Totota, Liberia (5:27)

1. *Identify when the soloist is singing and then when the chorus responds. Plot each of the turn taking or alternating and compare the relative length of the call to the response.*
2. *How does the soloist and chorus interaction compare to CD track 2 where the epic performer is singing with the chorus?*

Sang nong, o-yee.
Proverb child, oh, yeah.

Chorus: Oh yeah

Moses Woni, o-yee.
Moses Woni, oh yeah.

Chorus: Oh yeah

John Woni, o-yee.
John Woni, oh yeah.

Sakpa, oo-yee.
Sakpa, oh yeah.

Chorus: Oh yeah

Sala kpa kpa ba nya oo, ke nga tinaa lii nee po ee.
I'm a big, big sacrifice, but tomorrow I'm going to my mother.

Chorus: Ae-ee, nga tina li nee pona oo.
Aa-ee, I'm going to my mother tomorrow.

Sala kpa kpa ba nyaa oo, nga tina li nee po-ee.
I'm a big, big sacrifice, I'm going to my mother tomorrow.

After Moses had completed his opening verse, the chorus members responded with a chorus that was equally long compared to most other choral responses in Kpelle performance.

While the first occasion where I recorded the Woni group singing "Sala kpa kpa" was intended for the entertainment of workers in the rubber camp, I recorded this same song some months later in quite a different setting. The group had been called out to sing for the graduation festivities of the Sande girls of the Vai people living in Bookaitaa. This, as mentioned earlier, was the society that helped prepare young girls for adulthood.

> At one end of [a] narrow room sat three girls behind a table nearly as wide as the room. They sat on chairs covered with various cloths. . . . They were dressed in new dresses. . . . They wore rings, bangles, and long pendant necklaces. . . . Two girls wore clogs. . . . Two women who seemed to be hosting the event sat or stood up by the Sande [initiates]. . . . The performance began with "Sala kpa kpa," which seems to be the best known of Moses Woni's songs. There was no big preliminary introduction to it. The drum pattern played twice before going into the pattern. Also Moses did not do any extended narratives. . . . One of the things I had never seen before was his use of dramatic actions. . . . [He began the song by assuming] a Muslim praying position (Stone 1975:297).

Thus Moses had adapted to the Muslim-indigenous practices that intertwined in this event and made his entertainment music malleable to the occasion. I also noticed that he was very skilled at inserting Kpelle proverbs into his song texts as well as speaking with people at the event. Such adeptness brought admiration from the audience.

The Wonis' song texts were in Kpelle, but the structure of the music drew inspiration from a variety of other practices. In this case, the solo was not faceted, but rather extended and quite continuous. More importantly, the chorus did not break into parts, but sang together, sometimes in harmony. The emphasis was on a star singer and his support group. The group combined their voices in a very different way than the faceting evidenced in Kulung's epic performance. "Moses Woni certainly brings a performance that focuses on an individual in a way that no Kpelle music ever does" (Stone 1975:106).

In the epic, the pourer, who was certainly an expert and a soloist of sorts, was constantly creating a performance where the facets were prominent. Moses Woni, on the other hand, sang long sections where the chorus was silent. Then when the chorus entered, it sang a long section as a response to the soloist. The basic form was quite different. Rather than a tight cooperation among fairly equal parts, the soloist was much more highlighted and the chorus response enhanced the soloist.

The epic singer came from a milieu where famous performers must always fit into a tightly bound social fabric, where each person has a role and voice. In the Woni case, the idea of a star performer with emphasis on that individual emerged.

I learned about what they were thinking by playing back a videotape of their performances to them and then tape recording their responses. These responses explained a great deal. I also observed how involved they became as they watched the video.

> Our performance, the songs are in Kpelle, but the fêli (goblet drum) playing way, falls into Western performance a little bit. We told you that we heard the gbung-gbung (supporting drum) way of playing in Nairobi records. And we practiced it. . . . If you play it that way, a Kpelle person can dance in the Kpelle way, a Western person can dance a Western dance. . . . If I sing the song and they answer, I listen to their voice [chorus]. If someone answers, in a way that doesn't go on the path, I tell him, "You didn't do it well". . . . The chorus listens to the goblet drum sound, so everything comes together. If you delay the goblet drum voice, the singer will delay his voice. If you speed it up too much, the singer will speed up too much (Stone 1975:153).

Even with a star singer, the aspect of cooperation through performing fairly long facets was vital to the overall success of the performance. But the Wonis were tuned into the international popular music scene, and they implemented the idea of a prominent soloist from what they had experienced by listening to world popular music just as they had adopted elements of dress and hairstyle.

This music included some elements from indigenous musical practices. In indigenous Kpelle life, a musical soloist should never be too independent of the supporting singers.

Faceting music to the extreme degree required intense cooperation and considerable equality among the performers. The Woni ensemble showed how variations on faceting were present within their Kpelle performance and how influences from other popular music on the African continent—as well as Western influence—had produced long sections of performance and a lesser degree of faceting.

VOCAL AND INSTRUMENTAL FACETS
IN BUSH CLEARING SONGS

On the journey, the next turn was back upcountry on the main road to
Totota. From Totota, where I had attended market and heard Kulung,
the epic pourer, the journey followed a dirt road west toward the town
of Yanekwele (Figure 2.5). A mere eight miles away, the road had some
ruts and it was slower traveling than on the main highway.

I wound my way to this town whose name Yanekwele means near
the Yane (the creek that flows near the village and provided the water
supply for drinking, cooking, and washing). In a cove in the creek lived
several hundred catfish that are left undisturbed because the residents
of Yanekwele believe that these fish house the spirits of the village
ancestors.

I stopped in the town of Yanekwele, the place I spent most of my
middle childhood years. We came into Yanekwele as the sun was setting and people were returning from their farms. There was a larger
cluster of kids than we normally encounter because of Verlon's recent
work with the children of the town. [My husband had been filming

FIGURE 2.5   *Slit-drum ensemble from Yanekwele.*   *(Photo by Verlon Stone.)*

some children's games to use for his own research with school children in Totota.]

> People were strolling about, discussing events of the day. As usual
> . . . Zau and Yakpalo went off to make their social calls on people
> they knew. They went into Yakpalo's house to eat. Typical of the ex-
> change of information was the discussion in front of Yakaplo's house
> [concerning] his uncle who had been sent to Salala to build the dis-
> trict commissioner's house. . . . The discussion that ensued first in-
> volved only the family members. Then one or two other people came
> by to add their opinions. The town chief came over to greet me, but
> I noticed that when he heard the discussion, [he] walked away (Stone
> 1975:104).

Somewhat later we went to a nearby farm where a cooperative group of men, known as a *kuu*, composed of farmers, were working to clear the bush on a new farm (CD track 5; Figure 2.5).

ACTIVITY 2.5 *CD track 5: Bush Clearing, Yanekwele, Liberia (1:10)*

1. *How would you describe the call and reponse of the soloist and other singers?*
2. *How do the instrumental parts intertwine with this vocal singing?*

Such a clearing task occurred yearly, because each rice farm had to be cultivated on a fresh plot of the forest, one that has been fallow for seven years. I remembered several of the older men in the group from my childhood.

The men, armed with cutlasses (machetes) formed a rough line and each worked at cutting a little section. They worked to the rhythm of the slit-log ensemble, played by five men who weren't cutting. The slit log drum (*kono*) players each performed short patterns of several notes that interlocked with the other instrument's pattern. Layered upon the instrumental pattern, the singers also sang short patterns that inter-locked with one another. The people responding were both clearing brush and singing.

At the Yanekwele work site, some singers performed in the low pitch register, while others answered in a higher pitch register. Tokpa played the largest of the slit drums known as *kono lee*, "mother slitdrum." Moluba played the smallest of the slit drums, referred to as *kono long*, "child *kono*." The other players were Gbawong-pili, Kolee Gwii-meni, and Kekula.

The total impression of this performance was that there were many facets combined to create the overall *hocket* pattern. As the song proceeded, workers were encouraged to work harder by shouts from the nearby women who were preparing the food for later in the day. Thus, the facets of sound multiplied and the overall texture became more dense over time.

On another occasion when I watched members of a work cooperative clearing bush, I recorded this in my field notes,

The workers started up the hill brushing the low growing vines and twigs. On the left end of the group . . . instrumentalists . . . performed. Several people cut in front of them and cleared an extra fine path. . . . [One worker's work] was distinguished by a rhythmic coordination with the music. He worked much faster than the others, cut through larger trees than any others and seemed to more or less display his skills for everyone else. The music continued without pause as the workers [cut the swathe], which was probably eighty yards in length and twenty yards in width. (Stone 1975:140).

When it came time for the midday meal my notes indicate,

After some discussion, a procession of four women came with three large basins of rice with soup ladled on top. Five men grouped around the basins. They arranged themselves some ways away from each other, but each group was within earshot and conversational distance. Someone got spoons out of a bag and distributed them. One man had brought his own. People began eating from the edge of the rice nearest them. . . . The women bringing the food sat off some distance from the [men]. But people engaged in conversation as they ate. . . . After eating, people took pieces of meat and . . . sat back and enjoyed them. . . . The rice was not all eaten. . . . What was left was covered with leaves and set aside, for later I assumed. The head of the cooperative looked around and asked if everyone was finished eating. They all indicated that they were. Then he officially thanked the women who had cooked (Stone 1975:141).

The tight cooperation in producing the sound paralleled the human interaction that brought people together to work as a large group on a farm. The structure of the sound thus found an analogy in the organization of human labor. In the Wonis' performance, the solo singer was much more dominant and the chorus responded after more lengthy intervals than was the case here.

PARALLELS IN THE ARTS

The concept of faceting sounds or objects is one we can find in the related arts, not just musical sound. In Totota, the market town on the main road, the ensemble from Gbeyilataa assembled with their well-known set of performers. Master drummer, Kao, led the group, and his daughter, Keema, stepped into the arena to demonstrate her skills as a dance soloist. Her opening pattern consisted of short, diagonal steps forward and back with the right foot. All of this occurred at a very rapid pace. Kao explained that the pattern was indicated by speaking the syllables, "Keleng, keleng, keleng, keleng." The drum played the pattern that the feet were dancing so that we heard the rhythm as we were seeing the motion of the feet. The same held true for the dance steps that followed.

Now, in the dance Keema was performing, the pattern of *lôking* was always followed by the pattern *sokokpa*. First, the dancer continued to take short, rapid steps, but instead of moving ahead in a line, she moved in a circle with her hands leading in the direction opposite from her feet and body. Again it was fast, little facets, but now the dancer moved in a circular rather than a linear ground pattern.

The final pattern of Keema's dance sequence was known as *kenemâ*. This sequence consisted of a jump, then a step of the right foot behind the left, followed by the left foot moving next to the right. The right foot stepped in place, and following two jumps the dancer performed a concluding bow with the hands leading. Again, the building blocks of this pattern were small facets combined into a larger whole.

Each successive pattern became more multidimensional as Keema moved from the forward and back movement in the first pattern, to adding circular movement in the second pattern, and finally inserting the vertical jump in the final pattern.

At this point, you may well be asking yourself—how do we know that the Kpelle performers think of these parts, pieces, and patterns as facets that are then combined? What evidence do we have of their concepts?

I learned what some of the Kpelle performers thought about these patterns by playing back videotape recordings for the musician and audience members to watch and provide comments. "People I questioned had no apparent difficulty recognizing and identifying dance movements on the screen. . . . Some of the performers became so involved in watching themselves that they had difficulty making any comments, or made no comments the first time through. On later playbacks they offered comment" (Stone 1975:83).

I refer to these kinds of interviews as "playback" or "feedback interviews." They are occasions where people are presented with earlier performances and now, in a new situation, are asked to comment on what they experienced (Stone and Stone 1981).

FACETING: CUTTING THE EDGE

While I was doing fieldwork one day, I put on a videotape recording of the Gbeyilataa group. There was a section with Keema dancing the steps outlined previously. As the sequence of three patterns concluded, an audience member casually remarked "She's cutting the edge." "She's what?" I asked puzzled. "You know, she's cutting the edge," came the response. I wanted to understand what people meant by "cutting the edge." In this case I soon discovered they were referring to a faceting of the event, symbolized by the ending bow and hand gesture.

The bow and hand gesture at the conclusion of the third dance pattern created a feature that Kpelle musicians told me they prized highly and which symbolized faceting. This was particularly true of entertainment events where faceting was valued. Movements, like words, were combined and thought to have facets. As one singer explained to me, "we take one word, and we turn it, turn it."

CLOTH PATTERN

We can also look beyond musical performance events to the related arts to find evidence of faceting. Throughout West Africa, the cloth that is created shows evidence of faceting. First of all, the cloth woven on looms by Kpelle men from cotton thread is created in narrow strips several inches wide. These strips are then sewn together to create large cloths that are used for chiefs' robes or other important regalia.

Strips are one of the common units from which cloth is assembled. Blocks are another kind of unit that are placed on strips or large pieces of cloth. Kente cloth is a kind of cloth worn by rulers in Ghana, which consists of strips that are divided into smaller blocks. Thus, the whole design is built of many smaller designs and pieces, contributing to the total picture. Once the strips are sewn together, they are also offset to create yet further design units since there is frequently a deliberate slight offset of a design shared by two neighboring strips. Adinkra cloth, from Ghana also, is created by stamping designs into square block units, which are the building parts of the design.

Artisans also create tie-dyed cloth where the units may be designs other than strips or blocks. These may be circular or some other shape such as triangles. The most common dye for these tie-dyed cloths is blue indigo, which creates an overall blue and white pattern.

Yet another way that the cloth can be faceted is through embroidery. In this region, tailors are renowned for their skill in layering stitches upon the woven cloth to create curving and serpentine patterns. Sometimes the embroidery is so dense that it nearly obscures the underlying cloth pattern. But once again, patterns are layered upon patterns. Facets become the units of construction, and like musical sound, these small units serve to create the larger whole, whether it is a garment or a musical composition.

The most common cloth worn by Kpelle musicians in Liberia is printed in factories, frequently with designs selected for the West African market. If one drops in at the Wednesday market in Totota, one finds cloth sellers with their pieces of cloth laid on mats on the ground and draped from the sides of their stalls. Each cloth piece is cut to the size needed to drape the material around the woman's waist—about two yards. An array of bold colors and prints are displayed, many of them also faceted in patterns reminiscent of those cherished in the hand-created cloths.

As these cloths are worn, wrapped around the waist, the head, and sewn into bodices, they become part of the visual display at a musical event. As they move in dance, the faceted patterns worn by the performers take on yet a new appearance. The motion of the colors and patterns present a new incarnation of the shapes printed upon and woven into the cloth.

Cloth, like music and speech often carries lexical meaning. That is, there are specific meanings for patterns or designs. And the combination of these patterns communicates proverbs. Women most frequently choose to wear particular cloths at certain times to communicate specific messages. These patterns communicate messages in everyday life, for ceremonies, or other special events. Thus, these faceted patterns are rich in communicative meaning.

MASKS AND CARVED FIGURES

Dancers at musical events are often masked, disguising the identity of the person and embodying spirits who participate and communicate with the humans present. A number of peoples in West Africa carve these masks for use in their ritual life. While these masks are used in Africa in the context of musical events and are attached to raffia (a long, grass-like fiber) or cloth costumes, they have been extracted to museum settings all over the world and admired for their value as works of art.

If you examine the stylized representation of the human face portrayed in West African masks, you might notice that the surface is divided into multiple planes. On some masks from Liberia or Côte d'Ivoire, for example, the cheek is not rounded but angular, creating separate planes (Figure 2.6). Susan Vogel has noted for the Baule people of Ivory Coast that an important feature of the visual arts is its "segmented quality" (Thompson 1974). Senufo Figures, carved by the Senufo people, are well-known for their multiple planes throughout the carving as the surface is broken into many parts. Even the knees are bent, creating yet another surface.

This propensity to capture these facets artistically was fascinating to the European cubist artists such as Pablo Picasso. These artists proceeded to create paintings, inspired by African artists, that also broke the surface into multiple facets and then recombined them into a whole.

Visual faceting takes place across a range of artistic media and can be seen most vividly within masks and cloth from West Africa. There the multiple parts are deliberately created and much admired.

GREETING SEQUENCES

We can also look to language for evidence in the predilection of Kpelle people to facet. Take for example the greeting sequence, which people engage in many times each day. Notice the frequent turn-taking and the short phrases uttered by each speaker.

The pattern might proceed something like this:

A: Ba ung (Are you awake?)

B: Mm, Sumo. (Yes, Sumo.)

FIGURE 2.6   *Mask from West Africa: facets and continuity.*   *(Photo by Verlon Stone.)*

A: Mm. (Yes)

B: Ba ung, ee? (Are you awake?)

A: I koloi ponoi? (Is your skin clean?) [Are you healthy?]

B: Owei, kai fe Yala ma. (Yes, no blame on God.)

Each person has spoken three times in this fairly minimal greeting. And notice that one time the response by Speaker A said nothing more than "mm" to create a connection to and interlock with Speaker B. But again this faceting is valued and admired. People consciously choose to create the patterns in a way that is aesthetically pleasing.

Faceting reverberates throughout Kpelle life. It permeates different media and various activities. It is part of what makes Kpelle music distinctive and what is valued and admired in Kpelle performance. One should keep in mind, however, that other groups in Africa share this aesthetic value, so the Kpelle are but one representative group for us to study.

OBSCURING FACETS

For all the delight, which the Kpelle musicians took in creating facets, they had some kinds of music where the facets were deliberately obscured. Let's return to the earlier example of the epic. While the chorus and the instrumentalists created facets as was described, the epic was also considered a performance that has a quality of continuing forever. As one performer reminded his audience members, "You yourself the head of an epic does not come out [there is no cut-off cue], you just keep bouncing."

The pourer accomplished this hiding of the facets in a number of ways. First, a neat narrative conclusion was not reached. Just as Kulung was telling one episode, he inserted an idea and/or a musical motif from another episode. The hint about the stories of future possible episodes served to obscure otherwise demarcated facets. Second, the evening's epic performance typically concluded just as a high point of action was approaching. The audience was left hanging and anticipating more (Stone 1988:4–6).

In a similar way, ritual performance obscured faceting and always hinted at the quality of continuity. Thus, in one kind of performance, *koli-gong-song-pele*, when the dancer ended a solo sequence, he or she simply walked out of the circle, avoiding the bow sequence that Keema used for her entertainment dance sequence.

Koli-gong-song-pele was a performance that evolved during one of my field trips, and I was able to watch as a song brought to the village, was gradually elaborated with dance, and later embellished (Figure 2.7). As the event developed, gnarled pieces of wood were placed in the middle of the dance arena then used later by various performers even as lantern light cast the forms of the dancers in huge shadows throughout the village onto the thatch and tin roofs. This special performance was considered to be a ritual, addressing issues of witchcraft. As Kpengba from Gbeyilataa explained,

> This *koli-gong-song*, the way that song came to us is this. One woman, they were performing witchcraft. So she came out of her house in the evening. She stayed outside, and kept doing witchcraft, and morning

FIGURE 2.7   *Koli-gong-song performers, Gbeyilataa.*   *(Photo by Verlon Stone.)*

dawned, and all the townspeople had emerged from their houses. So there was no way for her to go into her house. She then leaped in the yard and said, 'Eh, morning has dawned on me.' And we took it as your song. Koli-gong-song, morning has dawned on you (Stone 1975:382).

So in the end, *cutting-the-edge* was a critical issue in music. Where performers employed it, entertainment music was dominant. Where performers didn't employ the cutting-off-the-edge, ritual was involved and continuity was an important emphasis in the expression. The chart below summarizes the contrasts.

	Entertainment	Ritual
Occasion	Performance at a market day	Graduation from Poro/Sande training
Facet, Aspect	Cutting-off-the-edge emphasized	Continuity emphasized
Possible Social Goals	Enjoyment, community interaction	Mark a child's move to adult status

FIGURE 2.8 *Facets and continuity in Kpelle performance.*

Faceting then becomes something definitive to Kpelle performance. When faceting is revealed, then entertainment is implied; when faceting is obscured then ritual is implied.

In order to learn about something so subtle, I not only attended many musical events, but I also carefully recorded people's speech as they watched playbacks of the video recorded performances. I transcribed and translated those comments and poured over them in search of clues for how Kpelle people think about performance. Amidst hours and hours of conversation I found wonderful clues like the "cutting-off-the-edge" remark. These simple words offered the key to a major aesthetic principle.

CHAPTER 3

Voices: Layered Tone Colors

∞

Just as the cloth considered earlier has design in the form of faceting, it also has color—vibrant blue, yellow, green, red, purple are part of the visual feast. Likewise, the musical sound has color—referred to as timbre or tone color. The color of sound is used to identify a person's voice on the telephone or differentiates the sound of a piano from a guitar even when playing the same pitch.

TIMBRE IN AFRICAN MUSIC

Scholars today realize that we simply need to be more aware of tone color in our attention not only to West African music, but to music of Africa in general. Many African musicians learn rhythmic patterns through phrases, known as mnemonic devices (memory aids) that convey timbre as well as timing. James Koetting, an ethnomusicologist who studied the music of West Africa in Ghana commented, "the importance of sonority cannot be overemphasized" (1970:120).

Roderic Knight, in his research of Mandinka drumming in The Gambia, feels that tone color is essential and that a drummer's skills involve learning to play "a pattern of timbres" (1974:29). He shows us just what he means when he isolates the strokes used to play in the *lenjengo* dance. Take the part played on the *kutindingo*, a conical drum that is played with one stick and one hand.

Kum is played with an open hand that bounces off the head. *Ba* on the other hand, sounds quite different because it is a dampened stroke, produced when the fingers hit the head and then press it to lessen the vibration. *Din* is an open stick stroke. *Da* is a dampened stick stroke. Thus, duration tells us little about all these complex timbres (Knight 1974:28).

People in the Kpelle region of Liberia pay close attention to the shading of sound and the various colors embedded within a performance.

Kum ba din   da

K   . B   D   . d

FIGURE 3.1   *Kutindingo strokes*

When I worked with Kao (Figure 3.2), the master drummer, he showed me how he could change the voice of his drum, depending on where he placed his hands, whether or not he cupped his hands, and what part of his hands he used to strike the skin.

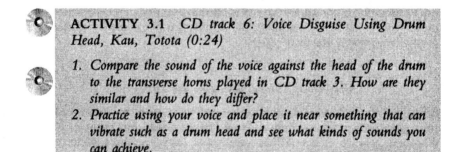

ACTIVITY 3.1   *CD track 6: Voice Disguise Using Drum Head, Kau, Totota (0:24)*

1. *Compare the sound of the voice against the head of the drum to the transverse horns played in CD track 3. How are they similar and how do they differ?*
2. *Practice using your voice and place it near something that can vibrate such as a drum head and see what kinds of sounds you can achieve.*

There is also a difference, quite obviously, in the tone color of the sound of Kao's drum and that of the triangular frame-zither.

The rich qualities of sound are prominent elsewhere in Kpelle life. Take, for example, the names of some of the months in the Kpelle calendar. The month that coincides with February is known as Nyéngnyéng, the name imitating the sound one hears when the dry leaves of the season crunch beneath the walkers' feet. The month of October, on the other hand, is Ngwee, the sound made by the bird known locally as Kpalo-ngwoni.

In story telling events, tone color helps to define a rich palette of ideas. The storyteller may indicate the sound made by boiling water: *fà, fà, fà*; he may show the way a boy runs: *kíli, kíli, kíli*; or he can signal confusion in a crowd *yuu-yuu*. In the first case, you might imagine the bubbles of water rising to the surface and then breaking at the top. *Fa*, with the "ah" sound nicely depicts that action. Whereas, *kíli*, with

FIGURE 3.2 *Kao Pee, master drummer from Gbeyilataa.* *(Photo by Verlon Stone.)*

the vowel sound as in "keep" signals a faster movement than the bubbling. Thus the vowel sounds or tone colors contribute to the meaning that is created.

Song texts abounded with vivid depictions of sound. As Feme from Gbeyilataa sang,

Ku baraa Kpela-pelee,
Our fellow young women,

Nga ngei te ngelei su, nga nyeng.
I raised my eyes to the sky. I lowered them.

Ngei ya e pu gata-gata ye gbai-kpang-su gbai.
My tears fell *gata-gata* like corn from an old corn farm.

Doesn't *gata-gata* portray a poignant image of large dropping tears?

At a performance in Gbeyilataa I expect to make a more detailed study of timbre—this very important dimension of Kpelle music making. As I leave Monrovia, the capital on the seacoast, I travel once again to Totota, the market town visited earlier, some ninety miles inland. A red laterite road a few miles farther leads to a little hamlet on the right hand side of the road.

I parked our Volkswagen bus, got out and started walking down the path that would, in about eight miles, take me to Gbeyilataa. As I approached the village, I heard drums and knew that I was approaching a performance that was becoming increasingly more exciting. I was first drawn to the sound of Kao, the master drummer's playing—he was playing the *fêli*, the goblet shaped drum (refer to Chapter 1, Figure 1.6). The patterns he chose were virtuosic, changing, and riveting. He was a man who in everyday life commanded attention—he exuded a sense of authority. He proceeded to explain how he could make his drum sound like almost any other instrument.

The *fêli*, was a single-headed drum with the head attached by a network of strings. What matters most, for our discussion here, are the rattles, metal in construction, which were attached to the drum itself. In addition to the basic sound of the drum's membrane being struck, I also heard the metallic jingling of the rattles, two very contrastive timbres. These layers of tone colors, however, were what delighted Kpelle audiences.

There was much more to the palette of colors in the performance of "Giing" as I heard it performed in Gbeyilataa (CD track 7).

ACTIVITY 3.2 *CD track 7: "Giing" (Game), Gbeyilataa Ensemble, Totota (6:12)*

1. *Listen to the "owl-raising-people" who add repeated short words or syllables after the song is established. Beginning at 3:00 write down the syllables you hear and note the time it occurs. Then note when new syllables appear. Plot the changes in the phrases as the singers create ever new tone colors.*

2. *Listen again to the song, beginning at 3:00 and clap one of the rhythmic patterns as you again focus on the "owl-raising-*

people." Observe the changing rhythm of the changing phrases
they sing layered over the pattern you are clapping.

3. *Listen to the beginning of "Giing" and see if you can identify*
   each time the two soloists (one male and one female) trade phrases
   within the piece and when this takes place.

While the *fêli* sound formed a series of penetrating mid-range to high
pitches, the supporting drum, *gbung-gbung* was much lower and less
resonant. The steady background beat was of considerably different timbre than the master drum. This resonant master drum sound contrasted
with the dampened timbre of the two-headed cylindrical drum (*gbung-
gbung*). One reason for the difference in the sound was that the *fêli* was
played with the hands, while the *gbung-gbung* was played with sticks.
Another reason for the difference in timbre was the type of skin that
was used for the head plus the degree to which the head was stretched.

The percussion section provided, at any one moment, at least three
contrasting tone colors: the *fêli* skin, played with the hands; the *fêli* rattles, shaken in sympathy as the drum body moved; and the *gbung-gbung*,
struck with sticks.

The voices of the singers demonstrated rich varieties of sounds. The
song "Giing" derived its title from the English word "game." Feme and
Yakpalo the two soloists, formed a kind of dueling duo in their vocal
depiction of a contest or game. The sound of the woman's solo voice
alternated with the man's voice. Punctuating all of this were the choral
sounds, short and regular, that paired with and supported the soloists.
The timbre of the chorus was reminiscent of the supporting drums in
its character of tone color that contrasted with that of the vocal soloists.

The *muu-siye-belai*, owl-raising-people, started entering and changed
the timbral structuring of the voices. They added ostinato patterns—
short phases that punctuated the performance in admired and valued
ways. As these ostinato patterns were layered, they could be heard as
though they were a single unit. In this case, there was a hocket effect
and the tone colors of rich hue formed the tapestry mix in this Kpelle
performance. The mixture became even richer as the performance proceeded and choral members improvised new patterns.

The privileged master drummer, Kao, improvised important shifts
in the sound. He played on different parts of the drumhead where the
resonance varied from other spots. On another occasion in performing

"Giing," he even paused and used the technique of "voice disguise," which created the sound of a horn as he placed his mouth close to the drumhead (CD track 6).

INSTRUMENTS: THE SOUNDS OF A TRIANGULAR FRAME-ZITHER

If a large ensemble has a rich palette of tone color, what can one expect from a solo instrument? How are the sounds conceived? In this region, the sound of an instrument is referred to as its voice (*woo*). The triangular frame-zither, *konîng* (Figure 3.3; CD track 8), is classified by the Kpelle as part of the *yale* or "struck" group because its metallic strings are plucked.

ACTIVITY 3.3 *CD track 8: Triangular Frame-zither (Konîng) (1:25)*

1. *Describe the way that the player shifts from playing in the higher register of the* konîng *to the lower register. To what extent does he alternate between registers and how often does he play in both at the same time?*
2. *Can you imagine that the player is creating one voice as the call and the other voice as the response in this example? Is the higher register the call or the response? Is there any point at which the "owl-raising-people" appear? If so, are they in the higher or lower register?*

Formerly, some chiefs had konîng players in their court. An old blacksmith from Gbeyilataa told me that when the founder of the town traveled, he took a *konîng* string player with him to sing his praises. I discovered a *konîng* player on a tropical evening in Totota. The itinerant soloist Flumo had stopped there for the evening and was delighting a small group that had gathered to hear him play.

What we quickly discovered was that this stringed instrument produced complex tone colors, not unlike an ensemble of many people and instruments. There were, of course, the strings producing a metallic

FIGURE 3.3 *Konîng, Triangular Frame-zither played by Wokpee from Gbeyi-lataa. (Photo by Verlon Stone.)*

sound, and metal rattles, just like the goblet drum, attached to the corners of the frame. One player explained why he added rattles (*nyeng-nyeng*) to the triangular frame-zither. *"I put [them] on there to make the konîng's voice sweet. To make the voice fine"* (Stone 1975:136).

Another aspect that altered the sound in interesting ways was the gourd resonator. This half gourd was held to the player's chest. As he played, the sound resonated or vibrated through his body, as well as the gourd. From time to time, he manipulated the sound by lifting the gourd from his chest briefly. As he did so, the timbre changed in subtle, but important, ways (CD track 8). The sound was more resonant when the gourd rested on his chest, less resonant when it was lifted off the chest on one side.

The strings were known by names associated with social relationships, much like the slit-drum ensemble. The lower-pitched strings were known as "voice of the chief" or "voice of the mother," and the higher pitched strings were known as the "voice of the child."

THE CENTRALITY OF THE VOICE

The sounds we associate with tone color are, for many Kpelle people, conceptualized as the voices of people. They are simply voices in a surrogate person. It becomes apparent that the basic idea of sound quality is derived from the human voice. For many Kpelle people, the voice is a concept that is prominent, whether an instrument is being played or a human is creating the sound directly. Within this concept, the possibility of variation is richly varied and nuanced. Richness is desired, attempted, and applauded within the timbral spectrum.

Players often develop a very close relationship to their instrument and some believe that the instrument activates them, not the other way around. As Bena told me,

> I find my songs from the konîng. The konîng raises the song. I sing it. It knows songs. If it doesn't show me songs, I won't sing them. If I raise it myself, if the konîng can't sing it, then I won't be able to sing it. . . . Here you are putting fingers individually and changing. That's what makes playing hard. It's in your mind, here you are coming to put your fingers there in order that those voices come together in order for it to sing the song. It's similar to the horn playing voices one by one. That's how the *konîng* is (Stone 1975:136).

INSTRUMENTS: MUSICAL BOW

The musical bow, *gbong-kpala*, which looks exactly like a hunting bow, is sometimes mistakenly taken to be a simple instrument. Looks are deceiving. Yes, there is only one string and, of course, there are no frets or bridges. But it's the mouth, used as a resonator that creates the endless richness of sound.

As the player encircles the upper end of the bowstring with his mouth, he forms a cavity in which the sound resonates. And here he can change the shape of his mouth to make strong overtones. The overtones are so strong that it sounds like two fundamental pitches are being played. But really, it's the overtones that are creating this wonderful illusion. So if you hear what seems like two pitches, it is a different aspect of timbre being exhibited. The fundamental pitch and the magnified overtones are heard together.

In this example of the playing of a bow (CD track 9), one can hear subtle changes of timbre that the flexible mouth can produce by changes to the cavity. The *konîng* player could lift his gourd resonator off his chest, but he couldn't change the fundamental shape of the gourd. But the bow player changes the shape of the resonator and provides an even richer palette for tone color change.

ACTIVITY 3.4   *CD track 9: Musical Bow, Totota (1:01)*

1. *Describe in everyday language the sound of the bow and then the changes that occur in the tone color. These are subtle and require very careful listening.*
2. *Listen for the moments when the overtones are most emphasized and it sounds as though two pitches are being played at once.*

In some places in Africa, the bow may be played with a gourd resonator attached. Elsewhere it rests on the ground and the earth itself becomes the resonator. In these cases, one doesn't find the flexibility that the mouth provides as a resonator, and subtle changes cannot be created with the same ease.

A very few fundamental pitches are played on the bow, but these represent more than a simple musical sound. They often communicate the phonemic or syllabic pitches of speech. In the Kpelle language, in which each phoneme is pitched, there are three relative pitches: high, mid, and low. High is marked (´), low is marked (`), and mid is left unmarked. Thus, the phrase, "Ngá ká a dung-kpúng-tàng-kpàng," (I'm a swaying thing) is performed as high, high, mid, mid, high, low, low.

The musical bow player communicates not only aesthetically pleasing sounds but sounds with lexical meanings, often based on proverbs. So word meanings layer upon tone color layers in a dynamic mixture—all coming from the deceptively simple looking one-string bow.

SOUND TEXTURE IN EPIC

Return to the epic performance which first introduced faceting, and examine that same example (CD track 2), considering tone color. As you listen again, notice the emphasis on sound texture or the combination of tone colors.

A part of each episode was spent on describing sounds or using a technique known as onomatopoeia. "Many things are imitated. In fact, each episode has a major thing imitated (*pokong*) and this imitation is repeated several times throughout" (Stone 1975:204). But this fifth episode, which is the focus of our example, literally exploded with attention to timbre. For in this episode, Woi's wife angered him, and was subsequently banished to the edge of town, where she was able to live by carving bowls with her voice.

She wasn't content to simply show the carving with a repeated word such as "chop, chop." Rather, an array of onomatopoeic words that highlighted timbral nuances were used, each depicting some new subtlety about the carving: *bongkai*, depicts the sound of a bowl with a large inside. (Notice that the "o" sound helps to depict the large inner bowl, and does so much more effectively than might occur with the vowel "i" or "e").

Kulung also used *kpolong* to mean "thin walls," or those that resonate when struck, *mono-mono* indicates "shiny blackness," and *fée-la*, conveys "smooth." These were all words that helped create a most beautiful bowl.

These beautiful bowls were carved by Woi's wife for male clients. But when, in the course of this interactive episode, a female audience member posed as a client wanting a bowl, a single word depicted the ugly bowl that resulted: *kpitili*, which means: thick, ugly." The jealous wife knew that she would not get any sexual favors from the woman.

The song texts do not necessarily follow a linear, chronological narration pattern. The text conjures up images and references known to the audience. Although the images and references may seem disjointed and unconnected to a reader from outside the tradition, they make narrative sense to the Kpelle listener and audience participant.

Here's how the episode unfolded on one particular occasion when Kulung performed.

Episode 5
Jealous Wife Carves Bowls (Stone 1988:28–32)
 SOLOIST: Ee-oo, bowl, mother, mother.

SUPPORTING SOLOIST: Ee-oo, bowl, mother, mother.

CHORUS: Bowl, mother.

NARRATOR: Only the bowl owner knows its price. I say, it is only the owner who knows its price. Oh, Maa-laa-ke-ma, we are going, ee.

QUESTIONER: From whose mouth is that song again?

NARRATOR: One of Woi's wives is there who is extremely jealous. He said, "Then let me take you from me. Go and sit at the fork of the road and carve bowls there. Everyone will be buying them."

QUESTIONER: They will be buying the bowls with what?

NARRATOR: They will buy them on the bed. That woman, you yourself know her ways. Oh, those who feed him say what? White bird knows its sitting tree.

0:47   *Bongkai, kpolong, kpolong, kpolong, kpolong, kpolong*

Kpolong, kpolong, kpolong, kpolong, kpolong, fee laa.

Koro, koro, mono, mono, fee laa.

Koro, koro, mono, mono, fee laa.

Koro, koro, mono, mono, fee laa

Koro, koro mono, mono, fee laa

Kalu fee laa.

Kalu koro, koro, kalu mono, mono.

Kalu bongkai.

QUESTIONER: Whose voice is that?

NARRATOR: Flat bowl, bowl well finished inside. Shiny black, shiny black bowl. Big bowl.

QUESTIONER: What does that?

NARRATOR: That's a bowl, oh. My friend, that is your bowl. Pass, let's go to the bed.

QUESTIONER: Is that the pay?

NARRATOR: I say to you, Woi's wife, her lust for men was great. She said to Woi, "You are not satisfying me." He said, "Then go sit at the fork of the big road." She sat at the fork of the road. You, yourself, Woi is a ritual specialist.

QUESTIONER: Yes.

NARRATOR: He said to her, "Just carve bowls with your voice." She carved bowls with her voice. But she carved bowls for young men. They just go to the bed.

QUESTIONER: Then is that the price?

NARRATOR: Then, that is the price.

Ee, Maa-laa, what did I say?

Ee-oo, Maa-laa, what did I say?

Only the bowl owner knows its price.

Only the bowl owner knows its price.

Sun-falling, Maa-laa, what did you say?

2:00   *Bongkai, kpolong, kpolong, kpolong, kpolong*

       Kpolong, kpolong, kpolong, kpolong, kpolong, kpolong,

       Kpolong, kpolong, kpolong, kpolong, fee laa.

       Koro, koro, mono, mono, fee laa.

       Koro, koro, mono, mono, fee laa.

       Koro, koro, mono, mono, fee laa.

       Kalu fee laa,

       Kalu koro, koro,

       Kalu mono, mono.

       Kalu bongkai.

       Kalu koro, koro.

       My friend, that is your bowl.

       Ee, my friend, pass let's go to the bed.

QUESTIONER: What!

NARRATOR: *A viking, a viking.* They have gone to bed.

QUESTIONER: Oh-koo.

NARRATOR: That's the price for the bowl. That's the song.

QUESTIONER: Kulung, don't lie to me in this place.

NARRATOR: Very close. Is that an untrue song I'm singing? If some of that song is untrue, then some mistake has jumped into it.

I, Tomo-catcher, keep your hand on the song. Sun-falling Maa-laa doesn't play,

Oh, only the bowl owner knows its price.

They greet that woman. They really greet her. The young men have really come.

QUESTIONER: What is the name of the woman?

NARRATOR: Ah, Woi's wife, she has no name.
Gelengoi, it's Gelengoi. And if Keapee would greet her, she wouldn't carve her bowl well. Greet the woman then.

QUESTIONER: I will greet her. Hello.

NARRATOR: Who is that? Wait, who is that?

QUESTIONER: It is I, Saki.

NARRATOR: Oh, Saki, why did you come?

QUESTIONER: I came for my bowl.

NARRATOR: Saki, greetings, greetings, greetings, greetings, greetings, greetings, greetings, greetings, greetings. Saki, what you all have done to me. A fine bowl is what you came for. Woi has long ago let go of me and dropped me. You yourself we were over that way long ago. You were doing that.

Respond to the song, respond to the song, my friend, respond.

Ee-oo, Woi has let go of me and dropped me.

Ee-oo, Woi has let go of me and dropped me.

Only the bowl's owner knows its price.

3:45   *Bongkai, kpolong, kpolong, kpolong, kpolong, kpolong*
Bongkai, kpolong, kpolong, kpolong, kpolong, kpolong
   Fee laa.
   Koro, koro, mono, mono, fee laa.
   Koro, koro, mono, mono, fee laa.

QUESTIONER: What is doing that?

NARRATOR: *Koro, koro, mono, mono, fee laa.*
She is carving the bowl.

   Koro, koro, mono, mono, fee laa.

   Bowl flat, bowl large inside, bowl well-finished,
   Well-finished.

   Eee, Saki, that is your bowl, oh.

   Oh, pass let's go to bed.

QUESTIONER: Oh, she has finished it.

NARRATOR: It is Keapee whose bowl matter is left here today.

   Oh, it is Malong-yaa-pu who is pitiful.

   It is Malong-yaa-pu who is pitiful.

AUDIENCE: Hello, woman.

NARRATOR: Who is this?

AUDIENCE MEMBER: It is I, Keapee.

NARRATOR: Keapee, why did you come?

AUDIENCE MEMBER: I came for a bowl.

NARRATOR: You long ago entered Woi's ears, he has hated me here, I have come here. I am here so that different men come, and is that why you have come here?

Kpitili, kpitili, thick bowl, don't come here again.

QUESTIONER: Hello, woman.

NARRATOR: Who is that?

QUESTIONER: It is I, Bena.

NARRATOR: Bena greetings, Bena greetings, Bena greetings, Bena greetings, Bena greetings, Bena greetings, Bena greetings. You came for what reason my people?

QUESTIONER: My bowl, I have been going with it and it has spoiled. That is why I've come for a new one.

NARRATOR: Oh, Bena, what you did to me is big, Bena.

> One single, single bowl.
>
> One single, single bowl.
>
> *Bongkai, kpolong, kpolong, kpolong,*
>
> *Kpolong, kpolong, kpolong, kpolong, kpolong,*
>
> *Kpolong, kpolong, kpolong, kpolong, kpolong*
>
> Flat, well-finished, shiny black, shiny
>
> black, smooth.
>
> *Koro, koro, mono, mono, fee laa.*
>
> Bowl flat, bowl well finished, well finished.
>
> Bena, that's your bowl.
>
> Oh, pass, let's go to bed, oh.

QUESTIONER: Thank you, for me.

NARRATOR: Dried millet, *wese.*

CHORUS: *Wese.*

Timbral nuance is at the very heart of this performance, and the tone colors of the voice give the woman her power to create beautiful pieces of visual art. One medium blends into another aesthetic medium almost effortlessly as vocal colors and visual colors are blended.

SOCIAL RESONANCE

Resonance, where sound is amplified, provides some of the dimensions of tone color that we experience. There is also a kind of social resonance that can be considered.

A good song ideally involves a large number of names, actors, and identities. These names through a single word often trigger a host of associations. Within a short period of time, a host of interactions are presented to the audience. . . . There is the ideal of resonance in whatever is done. Resonance of . . . aural sensations, visual sensations, and social chaining (Stone 1975:115).

The aural tradition is evident in the social aspects of life as well. What is true of the sound is also true of the social relationships among the Kpelle. Sound is multiplied and amplified just as social relationships are amplified in a kind of connection or social chaining.

I arrived at such a conclusion after a great deal of research and struggle with the concepts across the languages. Even though I spoke Kpelle fluently when I started this project, having learned it naturally as a child, the work wasn't easy.

Yesterday for the first time I felt I asked Yakpalo [my research assistant] some rather direct questions. . . . It was rather strange that finally I had a vocabulary that made it possible for me to ask questions that seemed idiomatic and Yakaplo replied in an idiomatic way. Yet I couldn't really write the equivalent of the questions in English beforehand. I took the few phrases [about musical performance] I had picked up in Kpelle and began asking questions with them. . . . It is such a tricky, delicate matter. You build with a few things once you have a frame that is correct and makes sense. . . . Now I can manipulate them with some ease (Stone 1975:115–116).

OTHER TIMBRAL DIMENSIONS OF SOUND

Musicians in many parts of Africa have a well-developed analytic vocabulary for timbre. It is important to observe how African musicians treat timbre since it is much emphasized.

These timbral aspects of sound extend well beyond music performance. I remember a high school student who worked as a research assistant in Liberia. He came one day with a Polaroid camera and said it did not seem to be working properly. As he described the problem, he said that earlier when he pressed the button to take a picture, it sounded, "kpi, kpi." Now he said, pressing the same button produced the sound, "kpung, kpung." He was relying on the quality of sound as well as the rhythm to explain his problem. Everyday life was often translated into and explained in timbral terms, a natural pattern for people who are so carefully and deeply attuned to the qualities of sound.

SYMBOLIC ASSOCIATIONS OF TONE COLOR

Kpelle musicians associate the colors of sound they create with a variety of spheres in everyday life. Often the sounds they create imitate the distinctive sounds of birds. This practice is not unlike the European composer Wolfgang Amadeus Mozart, who reputedly drew upon particular bird songs in his compositions—Kpelle musicians reference bird songs as well. One particular drum pattern that Kao, the master drummer employed, imitated the call of a particular bird with the phrase, *Kee kee zi-kee, zi-kee* (CD track 14). These were the syllables he spoke to remind himself of the pattern he was playing.

ACTIVITY 3.5 *CD track 14:* Kee kee zi-kee, *Drum Rhythm (:15)*

1. *Try clapping the rhythm the drum is playing as you listen to this phrase repeated several times.*
2. *Try saying the phrase kay-kay-jee-kay-jee-kay as you listen to the rhythm.*
3. *Listen to the changing tone colors of the drum part.*

Changes in timbre can also be important cues during performance that something is about to happen. When a performer shifts to a high falsetto voice and we hear, "Oo," this may signal that a tutelary spirit has made his or her appearance at a musical event.

If a vocal soloist changes timbre to a muffled voice in a variety of entertainment contexts, we should be alert. She may be shifting to sing about something associated with the Poro or Sande secret societies.

Timbral shift is the cue to help us know what is going to occur. The muffled sound is symbolically tied to these important Kpelle cultural institutions.

CLOTH COLOR

Visual color, as displayed in cloth, can be compared to color in sound, just as we considered faceting in both the visual arts and sonic arts. Cloth in West Africa in general, and Liberia in particular, shows this use of color particularly well. What is most striking is the use of multiple colors, often from complementary areas of the color wheel. Red is paired with green, blue with yellow, and purple with gold. As with sound, a multiplicity of color is appreciated and admired.

There is also an intensity of color in cloth just as we hear an intensity of timbre in the music. Pungent rattles are admired by performers. Bold color is considered aesthetically pleasing to artists in many parts of West Africa. Even if we like the music right away, we find ourselves looking and listening with new eyes and ears to try and appreciate what the people of Africa find pleasing, beautiful, and worth creating.

CHAPTER 4

Part–Counterpart:
Call and Response

∞

Music in West Africa has long been known for the call-and-response feature. That is, one performer or group of performers plays or sings first, followed by the second part, which becomes the response. This response is often performed by a chorus of singers or, more rarely, another single performer. Good examples of this technique are illustrated by the Wonis (CD track 4) as well as the group from Gbeyilataa, the latter featuring two alternating soloists and the chorus (CD track 7)

Around this basic concept, the Kpelle weave all kinds of delightful complexities. These exchanges between performers, taking turns in call and response, are the central focus of this chapter. Like faceting, call and response is another way of structuring performance that the Kpelle, as well as many other African and African-American performers, find aesthetically pleasing.

> One must always see the performers as reciprocal parts of a larger conception. Even the instruments are seen this way. . . . Music, as conversation, involves the aspect of call and response. The listener is expected to regularly make an audio response to the phrases of the speaker (Stone 1975:209).

CALL AND RESPONSE VARIATIONS

Call and response is employed in both vocal and instrumental music. "People directly state that the *fêli* (goblet drum) is like the solo singer and the gbung-gbung is like the [supporting singer]" (Stone 1975:155). Gerhard Kubik points out that xylophone players in southeast Africa sit opposite one another at the same instrument. The first player is known as *opachua* (the starting one) and the second player is known as *wakulela* (the responding one) (1965:36). In a very similar way, the *mbira*, a plucked idiophone well known in Zimbabwe is played by a single player. This player starts with the part *kushaura* (to lead the piece, to take the solo part) and then enters with *kutsihira* (to exchange parts of a song; to interweave a second interlocking *mbira* part) (Berliner 1978:73).

Nonoverlapping Call and Response.

Rice Planting Song. Among the Kpelle performers of Liberia, one can identify a number of varieties of call and response. In a rice planting song performed by women as they prepared the soil to sow the rice seed, the female soloist sang the call, followed by the choral response with no overlap (CD track 10). The women were in the fields where the thick tropical rainforest had been cut and then burned. They worked in a cooperative group to loosen the topsoil so that the rice seed would take root and sprout, using short-handled hoes to work. They bent over their work as they slowly advanced in a rough line of workers.

The soloist began singing a part that is sung to the text: "Oi-o-gbene-mei-o." To this the chorus responded, "Oi-o-gbene." As the soloist continued she began improvising a new line every other time. Thus, she varied her part some of the time. But the chorus was constant and did not change. Another voice was a woman on the sidelines offering encouragement to the workers. The shouts of the bystander were layered onto the exchange between the soloist and chorus.

ACTIVITY 4.1 *CD track 10: Women's Planting Song, To-tota (:48)*

1. *Listen carefully to the solo and chorus parts. After hearing them for a while, try singing the choral part, "Oi-o-gbene," with the chorus each time it enters.*
2. *Practice clapping a rhythmic accompaniment to the song in the rhythm that you might imagine the women are hoeing and preparing the soil.*

The work of the women, all loosening the soil simultaneously, was paralleled by the cooperation of the solo followed by the chorus, which they created with their voices. Therefore, physical work cooperation was fueled by the song. Their points of interaction were multiple, and song energized work even as work energized song.

Children's Counting Song. In another instance of nonoverlapping call and response, a group of young children visited the house in Totota, where we lived while doing fieldwork. They performed a counting song "One, two three, try it again. Fence two, three, try it again." (Fence is a term that often refers to ritual, since many rituals are performed within an enclosure fenced in to keep noninitiates out.) Here children had perfected the call and response structure. They, like the women planting rice, performed without overlap. The child soloist also varied her line even though the chorus performed without fundamentally changing their part (CD track 11; Activity 4.2).

ACTIVITY 4.2 *CD Track 11: Children's Counting Song (1:11)*

1. *Practice clapping when the soloist enters and then when the chorus enters. In other words, clap each time another group enters.*
2. *Now practice clapping in synchrony with the children as they accompany themselves.*

A group of young children had learned to create performance structures very much like the adults. Almost as soon as they could talk, they were singing in ways the Kpelle would consider appropriate. They had learned the timing and turn-taking of nonoverlapping call and response.

The balance in the length of phrases between the call and the response is a factor which one can hear. The women planting rice and the children counting all performed their call and response with a relatively equal balance between the length of the call phrase and the response phrase.

Kpelle Rubber Camp Music. Return to the Moses Woni song (CD track 4), which was mentioned earlier.

ACTIVITY 4.3 *CD Track 4: Woni Group (5:27)*

1. *Notice the nonoverlapping call and response in which the call, once the song gets underway, is very extended—an entire verse.*

The chorus is also very extended. One sees the possible range in call and response from short facets to very extended facets that alternate in this kind of structuring.

Some call-response phrases between solo and chorus are constructed so that the soloist has a fixed length and the chorus always responds after an identical interval. In other cases, the soloist sings a variable length phrase and must then clearly convey to the chorus when they are to enter. The soloist usually alerts the chorus by a descending melodic line, or by a decrease in the density of text or music that the Kpelle refer to as pulling, or injecting syllables like "ee" or "oo." Very frequently two or more of these cues occurred simultaneously, making the choral entry point quite obvious.

As mentioned earlier, there is considerable difference between the call and response of the Gbeyilataa singers and the Woni singers. The former have frequent exchange of call with response. The latter, in imitation of Western pop music have much longer calls and responses and much less frequent interchange.

Entertainment Love Song.   I recorded a woman soloist at one of the rubber camps near Totota, however, who sang a very long initial call, and then gradually shortened her phrase even though the chorus always had a short response. The text of her song caught my attention, for she sang of electronic technology and brought it into the text of her song, which also documented problems of love. She used the images of the gramophone and the telephone as she addressed another woman telling this woman to leave her boyfriend alone (CD track 12).

> I said to him, my friend and I were interested in the same man, when her mother saw this headtie, which I'm wearing because of the Loma person. I'm wearing this because of the Loma person.
>
> If the Loma person's name stays on me, I will not live. Gramophone, oh, come let's see it gramophone, oh.
>
> 0:20 (Chorus)
>
> Machines are endless in the Western person's home. Phone machines are endless in a Western person's house. Phone for me, I'll phone for you. Pass, let's see it.
>
> 0:41 (Chorus)

Overlapping Call and Response.
Musical Dramatic Folktale. (Chante Fable)   An overlapping call and response occurs in one musical dramatic folktale, *meni-pele*, which folklorists call *chante-fable*.

One travels some ninety miles interior to the now familiar market town of Totota and turns onto a side road and in another twenty miles is the well-known town of Sanoyea. (I say well-known because it lies on the path of an ancient trade route and is mentioned in many early accounts.) One of the families that has been prominent in this area is the Giddings lineage, a family that ruled (as chiefs) for many years.

One elderly member of the family, Peter Giddings, greeted us warmly and volunteered to perform *meni-pele* (CD track 13) or a sung folktale, also known as *chante-fable*.

This *meni-pele*, in contrast to the *woi-meni-pele* (epic) is a self-contained story whose plot is resolved in a single episode unlike the epic with its multiple episodes and very long form. Both forms include the ever-present chorus that performs multi-ostinato patterns as a background to the solo performer's narration, dramatization, and singing.

On that particular occasion, the gathered audience became Peter Giddings' chorus, and he taught them their part: *Go-go-yai go, go yai go.* They continued singing their part as a background to the song he sang. After he demonstrated one verse of the song, Peter portrayed the sound of the gun firing. He then moved to narrate the story, a tale of an orphan with a magical song. Now he overlapped with the chorus, which became a background multi-ostinato. But after a while he returned to the song and he performed the call and response structure by himself, since both the call and the response was of the nonoverlapping type.

0:33

PETER GIDDINGS: The child kept walking down the road, he kept walking down the road, daydreaming. He said, "What has happened to me is that I've lost my family. How am I going to stay alive?"

QUESTIONER: Don't lie to me.

PETER GIDDINGS: And so it was, he kept walking, and walking, and walking, and walking until the woman saw him.

QUESTIONER: What is going to happen?

PETER GIDDINGS: The woman saw that boy.

QUESTIONER: What will they do?

PETER GIDDINGS: The boy explained his plight.

QUESTIONER: What will the two of them do?

PETER GIDDINGS: The woman said, "Then I'm coming along with you." She came along.

QUESTIONER: What will she do?

PETER GIDDINGS: The woman had no family of her own. The child had no family. So they came together to share food. They were picking through palm kernels and she picked up the best ones.

QUESTIONER: What will she do?

PETER GIDDINGS: She gazed at one. She gazed at it and wished, "If only I were human, I could have it for a son."

QUESTIONER: What are you telling me?

PETER GIDDINGS: She traveled a little ways. The boy was calling. He said, "Mother wait for me." That palm kernel was calling.

QUESTIONER: Tell the real story!

PETER GIDDINGS: It had changed and it was calling, saying, "Mother wait." She waited and he said, "Now that we're together, mother, I can kill any animal in the forest. I use this song to kill it. If you sing this song, just let the animal come. But don't call a single wild boar."

QUESTIONER: Tell the real story!

PETER GIDDINGS: You yourselves know that the palm kernel doesn't like to eat the wild boar.

QUESTIONER: Tell the real story!

2:12

PETER GIDDINGS: [Song]

Oh, Nomong's rich child.
Your male equals have come here.
Who is my male equal?
Isn't red buffalo your male equal?
No, no don't compare me to red buffalo.
I've gathered it and dropped it.
Gili-kiting [sound of the gun], I've killed it.
(repeat song)

The story continued on for several more episodes with different animals appearing at different times. (For a more detailed discussion of this *meni-pele*, see Stone 1972).

ACTIVITY 4.4 *CD Track 13:* Meni-pele (Chante-Fable)
Peter Giddings, Sanoyea (5:56)

1. *Listen to the singing of the chorus and try to sing the ostinato pattern, "Go-go-yai go-go-yai go" with them as they perform throughout the narration and the song that punctuates the storytelling.*
2. *Another group in the chorus sings, "Ee nomo tolong, ee." This pattern fits between the other ostinato phrase, "Go-go-yai go."*

Try singing "Ee nomo tolong, ee" along with the recording or in alternation with a colleague who is singing "Go-go yai go."
Then you have recreated the call and response of the choral part.

In this performance, just as in the Woi epic, the voice possessed magical power. The boy was able to kill animals simply by singing a particular song and providing food for himself and his adopted mother. And the sound of gunfire was portrayed in the song with the onomatopoeic gun, *gili-kiting*, which multiplied the power of his voice.

The values of Kpelle culture were expressed in the way that people created this performance, revealing in the process, ideas about the concept and power of the voice. Both this orphan boy and Woi's wife were able to earn a living through the special power of their voices. Sound now exercised a supernatural power to provide food for them.

Epic Performance.   Kulung, the epic pourer, as he was known, was once again performing the story of Woi, that superhuman who was always moving his family. While there was much in the story that was fantastic and magical, some people believed that the Woi epic represented the saga of the Kpelle people who migrated from the north, coming from the grasslands and slowly headed toward the forested coastal area. In their travels, they met people who were hostile to having them settle on their land. So they often fought minor scale wars, analogous to Woi's little battles. Some time later they moved their people farther toward the coast.

Kulung was just beginning his fourth episode when I arrived at the gathered group, which was listening to and participating in the epic creation. One section of the chorus sang: *Vee mm, vee mm,* and continued without stopping. They were singing a continuous response. In this case their singing portrayed the sound of pumping bellows. *Vee* means "blow." The chorus was depicting the Tuu-tuu bird who pumped the bellows. As the story evolved, the needle that would be used to sew Woi's clothes needed to be forged. This iron needle was required to make his war jacket. So the first choral group kept the sound of the bellows going continuously while the second section of choral members overlapped with the bellow pumping sound and sang: *zang kali ma zang*. This latter group employed their voices to portray the sound of the blacksmith's hammer striking the iron to shape the sewing needle in response to the portrayal of the bellows being pumped. The first choral group illustrated the sound of bellows and was echoed by the second choral group, imitating the sound of the iron being forged. Thus, one choral group created the sound of air pumping and the other showed the sound of metal striking metal: two very contrastive sounds being portrayed by the music.

While the bellows were a constant sound and the choral group portraying the bellow sound sang continuously, the striking of the metal was periodic with some space for the blacksmith to reposition the metal before striking again. In this fourth episode of Kulung's performance on the particular day that we heard him in Totota, the two choral parts performed in overlapping response: The first response was not finished before the second response began. The two parts fit together with no space between the end of the first and the beginning of the second.

In fact, the overlapping responses were very much like a woodworker who creates a joint in the wood where the two pieces dovetail in order to provide strength to the joint. In the case of the Woi epic, the overlap created a close joining of the sound, making it difficult to discern where one part began or the other ended. This interlocking style was very similar to what Gerhard Kubik has identified as the "interlocking style," where each Mangwilo xylophone player in East Africa has his own part, but when the audience listens they hear the performance as one part (1965:39).

Earlier as I listened to Kulung perform, he launched into the episode in which Woi's wife gave birth to all living things (CD track 15).

> *2. Sing the song catcher's response, "Ziang kpono," as you practice fitting the two parts with someone else and experience how they fit together.*

A diviner was being called, as the episode opened, to predict when the birth would take place. The chorus sang: *ka doli e pa-oo* (Call him to come, oh), meaning they should call for the diviner. In between one choral part and the next, the song catcher (*tomo-song-nûu*) sang "*Ziang kpono.*"

Now the song catcher was a kind of supporting soloist who supported the main soloist as well as the chorus. The song catcher sang in the space when no other part was singing.

> **ACTIVITY 4.6** *Contesting Soloists and Owl-Raising-People*
> *If you return to "Giing" (CD track 7), a song you encountered earlier, you will see yet another variation on call and response. Here you encounter not just one, but two contesting soloists each providing a call with a chorus, then following the two soloists with a response. But very soon one hears yet more voices. Who are these people? They are known as the owl-raising-people who enliven and enhance the performance. The muu-siye-belai as they are known sing ostinati or short repeated parts and as the event begins (and as people are creating great music together), these people start adding their sounds. They seem to multiply as the event proceeds.*

The call and response became embellished with additional layers of sound that created the thick, rich timbred layers that are considered so desirable.

DIALOGIC RELATIONSHIPS

You might have wondered about some of the performers I've named as you moved through this journey. Who became the "questioner" or the "song catcher"?

Kulung found a questioner (*mare-kee-ke-nuu*) among the crowd to create a dialogue with him and ask the crucial questions. The questioner prodded the pourer, Kulung, at important junctures and urged him, "Whose voice is that?" or "Are you lying to me?" In a way, the questioner expressed aloud what many in the audience might be thinking, and thus became a voice for them. He often played this role with a kind of comic accent. His presence and speaking changed the narrator from being a lone speaker to engaging in dialogue at certain moments.

A dialogue or transaction then occurred between the two performers—even if Kulung occasionally played both parts. The song catcher (tomo-song-nûu) who filled in the spaces between the soloist and chorus, was a willing and knowledgeable volunteer from the audience who, like the questioner (mare-kee-ke-nûu), entered into a dialogue with the soloist.

The chorus was also carrying on a dialogue with the song catcher. In a similar way, the instrumentalists who were creating the interlocking metallic sounds responded to one another and to the rest of the ensemble. The complex dialogic pairings of the performers were as follows:

1. Soloist / Song catcher
2. Song Catcher / chorus
3. Soloist / Chorus

Within the Woi epic one might see a slightly different pairing of performers in dialogue:

1. Epic pourer / Questioner
2. Epic pourer / Chorus (with Song catcher and Owl-raising-people)
3. Chorus / Song catcher / Owl-raising-people
4. Instrumentalist 1 / Instrumentalist 2
5. Epic pourer / Instrumentalists

All of the performers also had a transactional relationship in a larger sense, with the instrumentalists relating to the choral group. Then, finally, the chorus and instrumentalists all supported and related to the singer who was the focal point of the event.

What becomes apparent is that soloists are not alone in their performance. Rather, soloists are balanced by supporting parts, creating a complex hierarchy of interrelated parts. Patterns of Kpelle performance are much like those of the *mbira* of Zimbabwe with the part that leads balanced by the part that follows.

RESONANCE

This call and response or part and counterpart relates to the idea of resonance that we encountered earlier.

> The idea of resonance involve the notion of things fitting together but being composed of many fractured little parts. That is, one does not think of one long note, but [of] many notes sounded in arpeggiated fashion to come together. . . . The size and extent of these unities can change. . . . In social relationships, people alternately delineate factions and relationships and the idea of [the] unity of people. You do not generally find one person speaking . . . and everyone responding en masse. Rather you have an intricate network of individuals resonating against one another and responding to create a larger unity (Stone 1975:154).

Drummer-Supporting Drummer. The part-counterpart pattern that exists for vocal compositions also holds true for instrumentalists among the Kpelle people as well. Master drummers among the Kpelle play the goblet-shaped drum (*fêli*) as mentioned earlier. These master drummers are the ones who play the flashy parts and lead the solo dancers in their intricate moves. The *fêli* is supported by the *gbung-gbung*, the two-headed cylindrical drum played with sticks.

The supporting drummer plays a steady, unvarying pattern, upon which the master drummer relies and to which he relates. This pair of drums then forms a part-counterpart relationship analogous to the epic singer and the questioner or the caller and responder.

The idea that drums converse is quite a common idea that African musicians voice (Chernoff 1979:53). They depend on another drum or several other drums and may find it difficult to play their part without other conversational partners present. They depend upon these other players to even think about their own parts.

GIFTS THAT KEEP THE PERFORMANCE GOING

Exchanges and transactions involve more than just the people performing music at an event. The audience may become involved in other ways, aside from singing in the chorus.

Pauses are important to musical events. These are moments when the singing and playing stops, and people give speeches to praise the performance or to offer gifts of liquor or money as an expression of appreciation.

It was a weekend evening and the rubber tappers had assembled to listen to a horn ensemble performance. After the ensemble began to mesh and the performance was moving along well, a woman stepped over to the master of ceremonies and asked him to stop the performance. He did so by raising his hand, as he stepped into the performance arena and blew his whistle. The horns stopped playing and the woman began to speak:

Kaa durii fee, ka seye, ka mama,
    You blowing the horns, thank you, thank you.

Naa ba Gamai,
    My name is Gamai.

Nga kula Gbonotaa.
    I come from Bonotaa.

Nga surong laa ba Kekula-polo,
    My husband's name is Kekula-polo.

So ka seye kpo kaa a damaa,
    So thank you very much,

Filei dei gbinii ngi su.
    In this Friday evening.

Gamai offered praise and identified where she came from and to whom she was related in order to give weight to her speech. Such praise encouraged the horn players to continue playing an even finer performance.

The important aspect of transaction had now extended beyond the performers to the assembled crowd. Performers were not just in dialogue between themselves, but very directly in conversation with the audience. In this latest phase, the audience took the initiative to communicate praise to the performers. This praise fueled the energy of the performers and assured that the singing and playing would be energized by the positive crowd response. The flair of the speech by the person praising the performers was very important.

Later that same evening another audience member Saki, stepped forward during a later pause. He praised the performance just like Gamai had done. But now he ended his speech by giving the performers two cents as he said,

    . . . ge ni dala ono feere ka ti.
        . . . then here are two hundred dollars.

The audience laughed at his exaggeration when he handed over a token two cents but called it two hundred dollars. Saki's gift and underscoring speech were very well received. The few coins were considered quite adequate to constitute a token that gave symbolic weight to the speech of praise.

These brief pauses and the praise that the audience offered were critical to the performance continuing far into the night. The audience let the performers know how they appreciated the music, and the performers were energized to continue. Later in the evening, liquor was among the gifts offered for the ensemble.

CHIEF-COUNTERPART

The part-counterpart relationship extends beyond music performance. The relationship is found within the social and political systems as well. The chief has his spokesperson or counterpart who works in tandem with him.

I traveled only eight miles past Totota, the market town, to the town of Yanekwele. It was a nostalgic stop for me because I had lived in this town as a child. As I crossed the creek right before entering Yanekwele, I recalled the raft my brother and I built and floated on the creek.

On that particular occasion, I went to the clan chief's court. At that time, the chief was Yaata, daughter of Bono-boi. Bono boi was the chief when I lived there as a child. While most chiefs were men, there were some women who served as chiefs in the Kpelle area.

We greeted Yaata and she regaled the people gathered in her court with stories of my antics as a child. The crowd was entertained, and even my husband chuckled as Yaata's words were translated for him by my research assistant Zawo Gotoko.

As we sat, the crowd increased, and Yaata prepared to hear a court case, for she was the judicial as well as executive official in her capacity as clan chief. As she spoke at the opening of the case, her spokesperson repeated her words nearly verbatim as he addressed the assembled people.

Why did this happen? We were capable of understanding what Yaata was saying. The spokesperson, or linguist as some West African texts call him, served as an intermediary between the chief and her people. In this role, he created distance between the people and the chief. He also enhanced her words by repeating them. Thus, in this formal setting, the chief was represented by a counterpart to the people. Yaata's prestige was increased as she used her spokesperson (see also Yankah 1995).

She continued in this manner until the formal hearing was recessed so that a witness who was not in the courtroom could be called. The chief spoke, then the spokesperson repeated the phrase. The chief asked a question, then the spokesperson repeated the question. The chief offered an opinion, and the spokesperson relayed the opinion.

This intermediary spokesperson balanced the chief and what she had to say. Therefore, the reputation of the chief increased as she drew upon the services of her spokesperson. It was like a call- response team where the response was an echo and amplification of the call.

I realized how important the counterpart role was as I delved deeper into my research. In the beginning, my research assistant served as my intermediary as we negotiated permission for me to record musical events. I thought to myself that soon my knowledge of how these negotiations worked would increase, and then I could speak directly to the musicians and their performance chief. But as I became wiser about how life was lived in the Kpelle region, I realized that it was advantageous to continue letting Zawo negotiate. My words and intentions were weightier with the help of a counterpart. Even if my language skills permitted me to engage in the give and take of negotiation, I should not change the part-counterpart relay of information.

All of this is so similar to the solo singer who, rather than stopping a performance herself, will ask the master of ceremonies to stop the performance by singing her wish in her song text. In the relay of commands, the soloist increases her status with the multiple layers of communication. Thus, what could be functionally simple is made complex for aesthetic and prestige purposes.

PORO-SANDE

The Poro and Sande societies are foundational institutions for Kpelle society. The chiefs defer to them, in making certain decisions, particularly those relating to the ritual and religious dimensions. Since all adults are expected to belong to Poro or Sande, these organizations are key sites for teaching values and rituals. The way Kpelle people employ these two groups is instructive for this discussion of part-counterpart.

At any point in time, only the Poro or the Sande can rule the land. Thus, if the Poro has control of the land, the men are dominant and will rule the land for the four years of the Poro session. During that time, young men will be taken to the Poro enclosure in the forest for initiation. At the end of the Poro session and a suitable period of rest for the land, the Sande society will be formally placed in charge of the land. They will rule for three years and hold the Sande initiation for girls in their enclosure. With Poro and Sande we have a part-counterpart in the world of ritual. They balance one another.

The association of Poro and Sande influence many life activities for the Kpelle. When a girl is born, she remains in the birthing hut for three days before emerging with her mother. A baby boy, however, remains in the hut for four days with his mother. Thus the ritual numbers of four and three become part-counterpart. And these associations continue to death when the death feast for a woman takes place three days after burial, while the death feast for a man occurs four days after burial.

The concept of part-counterpart is essential to music performance as well as to interaction and ritual activities. The concept extends beyond the arts to everyday and ritual life. The idea permeates Kpelle culture and is not limited to musical performance.

The effect of part-counterpart creates structure where individuals and groups, often very powerful, are always balanced by counterparts who share the role even as they enhance the other. The only area where part-counterpart has less importance is in popular music performance, which draws influence from Western popular music and emphasizes the star performer who is the center of attention.

CHAPTER 5

Time and Polyrhythm

∞

It is time to travel to Gbeyilataa to visit with the master drummer Kao. Gbeyilataa is an hour's walk from the main highway, on a path beginning just beyond Totota.

A MASTER DRUMMER'S LIFE HISTORY

Upon meeting Kao, I was struck once again by his presence. He was alert, sturdy, and thoughtful. When I asked him questions, he often paused for a time, and then he talked in a steady stream of words. Once when I asked him to tell me how he became a drummer he had this to say:

> I began playing the *fêli* (goblet drum) when I was a child. I began this work in Kwata. That's where we were when I started this work. It is near German Camp [the name of a worker's camp in the rubber growing region]. That is the area where I was as I began to get big. I was a big boy before we came to Yilataa. I started that work [drumming]. Our father was called Mala-yale Tokpa. If you hear that in Kpelle from a Zokele [northern Kpelle person] then that is a goblet drum player. As a young boy, I took old cans and hit them. And it was so—*mo to to to* [passage of time]. Where we were, I learned to play the drum for the horn playing ensemble. I really played the *fêli* in Kwalataa. And it stayed that way *mo to to to* [onomatapoeia to indicate the passage of time]. I was now a big small boy. I was really a *fêli* player (Stone 1975:61–62).

As we visited, Kao he began to show us his drumming patterns. First he spoke, "Kee, kee, zi-kee, zi-kee." Then he played the pattern that we can transcribe in the TUBS (Time Unit Box System), which has been used very successfully with African rhythms. In this system each box represents an equal duration of time, and the pattern would look as follows (CD track 14):

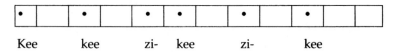

| Kee | kee | zi- | kee | zi- | kee |

I should point out that Kao himself used none of the quantitative patterns or notations that we rely upon. He spoke the qualitative, mnemonic syllables and remembered the pattern in which they were spoken. (These "mnemonic syllables," seve as memory aids.)

The pattern, as he spoke it, reproduced the rhythm of the drum strokes. The syllables and the different vowels also signaled aspects of the pitch or timbre of a drum stroke.

Kao told us that the pattern he was speaking and playing on his drum was the voice of a bird in the forest. Music was associated with nature sounds. The sound of the bird's "voice" as it was translated into verbal syllables provided hints about the timbre or tone color of the various kinds of strikes on the drum skin. *Kee* was more resonant than the syllable *zi*, for example.

The pattern that Kao had demonstrated was an interesting one. The reason it drew my attention was that it very much resembled a pattern well known among the Yoruba of Nigeria. The Yoruba speak their pattern as follows: *kong, kong, ko-lo, kong, ko-lo.*

If we depict it in TUBS notation it would look like this:

| Kong | kong | ko- | lo, | kong | ko- | lo |

Look at how close the pattern Kao showed us is to this pattern from Nigeria if we place them next to one another.

| Kee | kee | zi- | kee | zi- | kee |

| Kong | kong | ko- | lo, | kong | ko- | lo |

The only difference in striking patterns is that while there are two strikes on *ko-lo*, there is only one strike on *kee*. Otherwise, the patterns are identical. Compare yet one more pattern with these two. The third pattern comes from the Ewe people of Ghana and it appears as follows:

| • | | • | | • | • | | • | | • | | • |

The only difference found in all of these patterns is a variation in the last three boxes. Thus, we find a pattern that is, in essence, the same throughout vast reaches of West Africa.

ACTIVITY 5.1   *Timelines and Mnemonic Syllables*

1. *Practice saying the illustrated timelines in rhythm while you clap them.*
2. *Next, play a steady background pattern, one for each of the TUBS boxes with the right hand while you play the timeline with the left hand. Be sure to keep a steady pattern.*

This pattern, whether found in Liberia, Nigeria, or Ghana, fits, of course, with other patterns played at the same time. This particular pattern is known as the "timeline," "structural core" (Kubik 1983:38), "time-keeper" (Nketia 1958:21), or "standard pattern" (King 1960). Therefore, it has a role in keeping everything appropriately linked. Players use it as a reference point to synchronize the drum, bell, and vocal parts. The timeline is one of multiple reference points upon which musicians rely.

Significantly, the pattern is played in Africa without any reference to the counting or the quantitative means that Western art music might employ. People in the West frequently favor a quantitative approach, while the Kpelle—and many other peoples in Africa, as well as in places like India—employ the syllables that are spoken in qualitative relationship to one another.

Roderic Knight reminds us that timbre is important to understanding rhythmic patterns. He states, "In view of the importance of timbre in the drumming technique, one may conclude that his [the drummer's] abilities are at least in part attributable to learning each rhythm as a pattern of timbres" (1974:29).

If you look around even further in Africa, you observe that this timeline is found even more widely. Following are examples of the pattern as it appears in the music of the Mahi of Dahomey, Tanzanians singing in Swahili, the Hausa of Nigeria, the Babanzele people of the Central

African Republic, and circling back to West Africa, the Mende people of Sierra Leone. Observe the similarities and slight differences in the patterns.

Kpelle—Liberia

Ewe—Ghana

Mahi—Dahomey

Swahili—Tanzania

Hausa—Nigeria

Yoruba—Nigeria

Akan—Ghana

Babenzele—Central African Republic

Mende—Sierra Leone

All of the patterns coincide on the first, third, and tenth unit. In between there are some variations. If you try, using quantitative logic, though Kao or other drummers in Africa would not likely think this way, consider grouping the inner parts into some kind of subpattern. Note these points.

Begin with Kao's pattern:

Kee   kee   zi - kee   zi -   kee

| • | | • | | • | • | | • | | • | | |

If you look at the words and the underlying duration, you see that *kee* consists always of two units and *zi-kee* of three units, for a total of two plus three units. Thus you have a pattern of 2 + 2 + 3 + 2 + 3 for the entire phrase. The whole pattern is built of asymmetrical groupings juxtaposed with symmetrical. One further grouping would be to consider that there is a grouping of 7 + 5, and, finally, the total pattern consists of twelve units.

| • | | • | | • | • | | • | | • | | |

Kee   kee   zi - kee   zi   - kee
2   +   2   +   3   +   2   +   3
7   +   5

Now, all this looks and also sounds quite interesting. As you move along after the two *kee*'s you think that you understand the familiar beat. Twice the shorter value, then a longer value. Some ethnomusicologists, discerning this combination of two followed by three refer to this as hemiola, in this case horizontal hemiola. (Hemiola simply means the play of a two-based pattern against a three-based pattern either horizontally or vertically.)

Another example of horizontal hemiola could be as follows:

| • | | • | | • | | • | | | • | |

2   +   2   +   2   +   3   +   3

Here the larger grouping of 6 + 6 is symmetrical.

The timeline pattern in West Africa is often played on a double bell. Other times it is simply played on a shaped piece of iron. The Kpelle strike a boat-shaped piece of iron called *kone*. In Ghana and Nigeria, however, a double-flanged bell is struck. In both cases the timbre of the struck metal is distinctive and rather penetrating. In the epic performance, players created a sound very similar by striking beer bottles with the back edge of a pen knife (CD track 2).

FITTING THE PIECES TOGETHER

As you begin to check the placement of one part against another in relationship to the timeline, you discover an important rule. The parts fit together like a jigsaw puzzle. That is, there is one, and only one, placement according to the musicians with whom I've worked. In other words, it matters a great deal how each part aligns with the other. Each part is a distinctive rhythmic pattern that fits in one, and only one, precise way with the other parts.

In other ensembles, as you listen, notice the way the parts fit together. With each part having a distinctive pattern, you obtain several interesting effects. First, you have polyrhythm or, literally, many rhythms. Secondly, you experience vertical hemiola or the vertical placement of 2 against 3. You appear to be moving together in 2's when a 3 displaces the whole arrangement and the wonderful tension of 2 against 3 appears. The tension is not with a central underlying beat, but with the different adjacent parts. As the late John Blacking stated quite appropriately,

> [W]hen it is played in Europe it is always conceived as the product of a single agent—with a very few possible exceptions. . . . In the African context the rhythm expresses the perfect cooperation of two performers who nevertheless preserve their individuality by maintaining different main beats (1969:18).

A former student of mine, Alain Barker, compared the use of some Western rhythmic patterns based on an organized down beat or conductor's beat to a house built on a concrete foundation. All parts relate to and depend upon that anchoring point in the ground. He contrasted that to African performance, which uses different organizing beats and is like a tent. The stakes in the ground hold ropes that depend upon tension between them to hold up the structure. African performance frequently depends upon multiple points of organization rather then a singular focus.

The patterns we have been considering up to now form the basic fabric of the performance. They are rather fixed and invariant. But there is yet more to come. The one part that varies is that of the master drummer. The finishing touch is the master drum and the improvisation that the master drummer creates against the rich, but stable backdrop of the supporting instruments. The master drummer must understand fully how each part interlocks with the whole in order to select from a repertoire of short patterns to improvise appropriately. It is that skillful composing of musical ideas as he plays that puts the final touch into the rhythmic weave that we experience. We may know and recognize the small patterns, but we don't know how the master drummer is going to place them together. He composes on the spot, and we are wonderfully surprised.

The vocal soloist, just like the master drummer is expected to constantly change and vary his or her part. He or she has the freedom or the license to change and layer sound on top of the sounds that the other performers have carefully crafted.

RHYTHMIC PATTERNS IN THE EPIC

Consider the kinds of rhythmic patterns that emerge in the music and text of the epic (CD track 2). In Episode 1 the two bottles being struck were playing in a vertical hemiola.

Contingency.   There are certain patterns that emerge in the epic performance, which depend upon particular circumstances and may change from one event to another. The episodes of the epic are not necessarily performed in chronological order. In other words, one day Kulung may begin in the middle of Woi's life, return to his birth and then move to yet another period in his life. On another day the episodes may be performed in quite a different order.

Why perform epic in such an apparently strange way? For the Kpelle, you need to explore the logic that permits such an ordering. First, the Kpelle say, epic is eternal—it never ends. And thus no single performance can encompass the total epic. One simply explores bits of the total epic at any event. No attempt is made to move in a kind of developmental sequence. Instead, you move around in time, being reminded at various moments of one episode or another to which the power may wish to move later.

I like to think that Kulung is "moving down a path" as he creates epic. He flits from one topic to another, and never spends too much time in one spot. In his second episode (CD track 14), for example, he begins with the following performance:

Episode 2

<table>
<tr><td></td><td></td><td>Song</td></tr>
<tr><td></td><td>Narrative</td><td></td></tr>
<tr><td>Epic framing</td><td></td><td></td></tr>
</table>

KULUNG: My fellow, answer man, answer man.

> It's the diviner of the hole that they are calling.
> It was Woi's wife who was pregnant, and they
> are calling the diviner from the anteater's hole.

You, yourself, the head of an epic doesn't come out. You just keep bouncing.

> They are going for divination. And the diviner
> of the anteater's hole is in the road. He comes
> to him, and says to him,

> "Then here I am."

> "Come and divine for me."

>> Ee; what does Maa-laa-ke-ma say?

>> Go, call the diviner of the anteater's hole to come.

>> Go, call the diviner of the anteater's hole to come.

Boys answer, boys answer, boys answer. Take your hand out of your mouth.

>> Oh, what does Maa-laa say?

Woi's wife was pregnant kpung-kung. And that is why they are going for divination.

QUESTIONER: What did you say?

>> Kulung: They have gone to the diviner of the anteater's hole. He said, "Then, that's fine. Oh, the pregnant woman coming for divination? Then it is a matter that . . . so, ah Woman." He

said, "Then woman . . . she will give birth right now. Just cut a road."

At that time there was nothing alive. Sheep didn't exist. Chickens didn't exist. There was nothing at all alive.

Q: Are you telling the truth?

KULUNG: Very close.

Ah-oh, what does the diviner say?

Go, call the diviner of the anteater's hole to come.

I tell you the stomach. They said, "Cut a road." The woman was delivering I tell you. People are coming, chickens, ducks, sheep, goats, all, all are coming. The only things left are Spider and Slit-Drum. Slit-Drum has come.

Q: My friend, what are you telling me?

KULUNG: Keng-keree, eh.

Dried millet, wese.

CHORUS: Wese.

Kulung moves very quickly from a direction to the chorus when he says, "My fellow, answer man, answer man," to narrating the story, "It's the diviner of the hole that they are calling." He then explains the structure of the epic to the audience, "You yourself, the head of the epic doesn't come out," then proceeds back to the narration, "They are going for divination . . ." afterward he moves to the more reflective song, "Ee, what does Maa-laa-ke-ma say?"

He began the experience by establishing the frame of the epic or setting up the structure, then he started telling the story. Next he returned to framing the epic before moving back to telling the story. Finally, he sang the song, which was the most reflective aspect of the epic.

Kulung never stayed with any one aspect too long. He kept moving back and forth between framing, narrating, and reflecting (through the singing of the song). The shift from narration to abstract song, and from narration to direction for the chorus actually presented different vantage points or perspectives. They were all dimensions of a kernel idea.

Once the key to the episode has been discerned, then it is apparent why the narrator has allowed two apparently dissimilar concepts to coincide. Now, the audience recognizes a new perspective on meaning. In the bowl carving episode that was considered earlier, the sounds of carving a beautiful bowl were juxtaposed upon carving an ugly bowl. The theme of jealous co-wives recalls an area of great concern and attention in everyday Kpelle life. Kpelle men may have more than one wife, and these wives must learn to coexist peacefully, if not happily. This theme convened in the epic speaks of getting along. The bowl carving incident has both entertained and made a point for the audience to remember.

Action.   One of the key aspects of the narration was action. It was first revealed in small sections such as the rich, varied chopping sounds. But what is soon realized is that just as the episodes were not chronological, the action also did not lead to one major climax. As the house confronted obstacles, Woi overcame them and moved on.

This lack of linear progression in the Woi epic, as in some other African epics, can be compared to the situation in Javanese shadow puppet theater (*wayang kulit*). A *wayang* plot is built on coincidence and may begin at any point in the story in terms of time. But the action does not occur with a sense of linear progression, and does not lead to one major climax. Alton L. Becker claims that in order to focus on, for example, causal sequence and character development is to miss the area of relevant variation in *wayang* theater and to miss the subtlety and depth of a good *wayang* (1979:219). In a comparable way, Robert Plant Armstrong describes the episodes of the Nigerian musical drama, *The Palmwine Drinkard*, as "sequential" rather than "consequential" in what he terms "intensive continuity." He goes on to say that, "continuity can be seen as a function of the density of multiple, discrete parts" (1971:168).

The Woi epic episodes are ordered by decisions that may vary the order from one performance to another. What matters immensely is that an idea within one episode is presented that shows some evident connection to another episode. Just as the drum patterns interlock like pieces of a jigsaw puzzle, pieces of the epic also interlock in the manner of puzzle pieces. But in the case of epic, the episodes have multiple interlocking possibilities, just as the master drummer has the flexibility to vary his presentation in regard to the other parts.

Here is what creates continuity: Kulung helps intensify the connections by hinting at a possible, upcoming episode with a musical or textual clue. But Kulung teases the audience, often offering multiple clues so that we can't be sure which path he will ultimately take until he actually does so.

INNER TIME

Kpelle Performance in Liberia. We have been talking about the nuts and bolts of building rhythmic patterns in African music. But you might ask, what about those aspects of time, which are more difficult to describe via words? Once an ensemble synchronizes all the parts, and listeners or dancers become completely involved in the music they are making, another kind of time becomes important. Perhaps you can think of a situation where "clock time" or "outer time" quit being important for you and "inner time" or a qualitative time became much more important.

This is really the soul of time and that place where people experience a "flow" or a "high." What can we say concerning that type of rhythmic and temporal experience? Ethnomusicologists, among other scholars, call this area of music "inner time" and in that arena a very special awareness is experienced by performers and audience alike. The Kpelle describe a performance that has really coalesced so that the experience of inner time may emerge as, *"goo a pilang"* (the foot has stepped down). The performers and audience then perform together in a tight synchrony that sets the stage for inner time to emerge. It is the aspect that the Kpelle refer to as making performance "one."

Inner time for the Kpelle occurs during the next stage: *maa-ygee* (selecting). Here the participant, in a kind of stream of consciousness, gains new awareness of the event. As I have stated in other writings "The whole *maa-ygee* phase of an event or song presents a multiple image of the idea being communicated through music performance" (Stone 1982:107). The listener, now tuned in with the forward motion of the music can move into flights of experience that are free from the constraints of outer, chronometric time.

The Island of Lamu, East Africa. This need for tight coordination as a way of setting up the experience of inner time is described by Alan Boyd while working in the Muslim community of Lamu, Kenya in East Africa. Participants sing in unison and sway together as they move toward inner time (1977:8). Volume, intensity of the beat and the tempo all increase as they move to the end of the verse. People are entering an experience of inner time.

The Shona of Southern Africa. This move to an inner time experience or flow was apparently evident in Paul Berliner's description of an *mbira* player, though he didn't use the term inner time. The whole event happened at sunrise following an all night ceremony to communicate with ancestors. One *mbira* player, Hakurotwo Mude, was seated and played quietly as he gazed off in the distance. He didn't even notice his young son putting his hand on his father's shoulder.

> As Mude played the *mbira* his eyes became clouded. Tears welled up and fell silently down his cheeks. It was some time before anyone noticed what was happening. Finally, Mude's father-in-law walked over and knelt before him. Careful not to interfere with the playing of the *mbira*, the old man pulled a handkerchief out of his pocket and blotted up the tears on Mude's cheeks. Tears flowed so steadily that the old man saw it was to no avail. He stood up and silently motioned to all the other villagers seated around to follow him into the large kitchen where the bira ceremony had previously been held. So as not to embarrass Mude, we left him to his music and his tears. (1978:132)

Though we can't know for sure, or examine Mude's mind directly, he seemed to be moved by his music to a deep emotional experience that most likely took place in inner time. He was not thinking about the mechanics of creating the music, or the social scene in which he performed and both of which he would most likely experience in outer time. He was moved rather in a very emotionally charged way by his experience.

Somewhere in the inner time experience, people undergo what is known as an altered state of consciousness. Their body processes may be radically changed. They may show different dance patterns, convulsive limb movements, and a change in eye focus.

The Spiritual World. A number of West African peoples believe that a deity possesses the person, and the deity then controls the actions of the person. This all happens in a very deep state of inner time, and it is considered a really high point for the dancer. This possession is valued for communication or for healing and seen as a very positive experience.

Though it is beyond the scope of this book to provide details about possession in music performance, there is a need to explain it in relation to inner time. "The paradox of the musical experience appears that the more deeply one experiences inner time, the greater the danger of losing awareness of the outer time and coordination necessary to continue the event" (Stone 1988:80). So inner time and outer time blend in a very delicate balance to create an event that involves both human and, sometimes, spirit participants.

THE LARGER PROCESS

A larger process of layering rhythm can be discerned in West Africa. Songs, events, and musical pieces all begin with staggered entrances. (The epic performance of the Kpelle is but one example as heard on CD track 2.) One part enters, and then another. The parts perform together as they "tune in" to one another, shifting and adjusting their musical concepts to mesh into a tight unit. They search to find the best fit until, like a three-dimensional jigsaw puzzle, the pieces neatly align with one another. Then other parts enter and they too, adjust to one another. Consider how different this is from some orchestras in Europe and the United States where the conductor raises his baton and the ensemble relates to a focal leader for the rhythm.

In West Africa, the ensemble often gradually synchronizes parts that are carefully defined—each part with a distinctive rhythm fitting together with other patterns in a prescribed way. These instruments and/or voices create the rhythmic foundation in outer time against which the controlled creativity of the solo singer, dancer, or drummer unfolds. In the next phase, the audience is prepared for the experience of inner time where a kind of flight of fantasy develops as the tight synchrony now promotes this individual flow, even as everyone remains keenly aware of one another.

"Making music one" moves to "making music many" where the deepest and most profound emotional experiences in music occur. Individuals might move in and out of these phases at any time, but they are more or less experiencing this progression along with the other participants. A complex setup of asymmetrical patterns with all kinds of timbral and pitch complexities played at, what will seem to most of us, very fast tempos creates experiences that are difficult to translate into words.

As one Kpelle proverb explains: performers are compelled by the music to dance. They can't help themselves and, in fact, should respond to the music. *Māla-nuu va too a ygene, ge ni a m la tong tee* (A dancer doesn't just stand outside, otherwise she/he has broken the dance law).

People may feel compelled to begin dancing or moving as they hear these sounds, particularly as they become ever more finely tuned to one another. The compelling nature of West African music is that it is created in time and moves the audience and performers alike, ever closer to an inner time experience where the mechanics fall away and the flow of time overtakes the people. Through excellent music making, performers beckon the audience to respond and become involved. The audience has learned to react to particular sounds and rhythms from early childhood onward. They may become dancers or chorus members. They may offer gifts to the performers to encourage ever finer playing, and often accompany it with a speech. These gifts may be quite lavish due to the fact that audience members are deeply moved by what they have experienced.

Among the Kpelle of Liberia (as well as Africans across the continent) time is a complex issue in regard to music performance. Within a single performance, a rich temporal variety emerges.

LIFE HISTORY

The epic power and the master drummer are licensed to creatively improvise their patterns. Other aspects of Kpelle life include analogous patterns. A life history is an elaborate account that a person constructs for the researcher. In this case, the musician chooses how to present herself or himself, what to tell and when to tell it.

In my study of Kpelle music, I sat down with several key musicians and tape-recorded what they told me about their lives. These conversations lasted a number of hours and were later transcribed into Kpelle and then translated into English for my study. Remember that you found the Woi epic was narrated in a nonchronological sequence? Well, I discovered that all of the life histories I recorded were also nonchronological without exception. People moved from one life episode to another, triggered by memories. The life stories did not proceed from birth onward to maturation. Kao, the drummer, for example, provided a thumbnail summary of his life in his opening statement.

> I was born in Mopaitaa, Kanema. But I was in Yilataa when I reached puberty and got a wife who had the children here. But I stayed there and I said, "I am going to my brother." He is the only one—we can sit and think of each other. That's why I went to him. I've spent two years in Pee. This is the second finishing here.

His next statement was reflective as he talked about his mother's name, as well as his older brother. But the statement that followed that one was an account of how he learned to play the drum, with a return to his childhood in the narration.

What the Kpelle audience experienced here was an avoidance of linear progression in a way that is very similar to the epic performance. The actions in this life history narrative were linked more by association than causation.

TIME IN LOCAL LIFE

People in the Kpelle rural areas define time through shared experiences with other people. They identify these moments as "Tolbert's government," "market day," "rice harvest," or "Zau's death." Even seasons coincide with the harvest or planting rather than being cause for rice to be planted or harvested. As the Tiv in Nigeria stated, "The first harmattan comes when we cut guinea corn" (Bohannan 1953:255).

This pattern extends even to Algeria in North Africa where the Kabyle pray five times a day as part of their Muslim religious practice. As Pierre Bourdieu explains, "The islands of time which are defined by these landmarks are not apprehended as facets of a continuous stream, but rather as so many self-enclosed units. . . . Each of the temporal units is an indivisible block juxtaposed to the others" (1963:59).

Months for the Kpelle have qualitative names. And these qualities are those that coincide with social action at specific moments. There is the month of hoe grass, mist, or *ngwee* (the voice of the bird that appears in that month), among others. Whether the leaves are crunching, the birds are singing, or the mist is falling, sound qualities dominate the names of the months.

A fascinating point is the way a year is regarded. The Kpelle term for year is *korang*, which is the same term as fence. And a fence around a rice farm encircles or encloses an area. Thus a year contains or encloses social action that is part of a year. It's not a progression of days moving from the past proceeding into the future. Furthermore, as mentioned earlier, "fence" is the term associated with performing ritual. So action, particularly that involving social interaction, is critical to the definition of a year.

BALANCING THE QUALITATIVE
AND QUANTITATIVE

In Kpelle everyday life, the concepts about time and its character relate very closely to music performance. There is considerable consistency between the way that many Kpelle people structure their lives in musical performance as well as in their everyday activities.

The way people talked about and organized daily life and music de-
pended more on the qualities of interaction than upon quantitative time
reckoning with clocks or metronomes. Yet as the Kpelle, like all of us,
moved into the Internet age, they continued to juxtapose qualitative
with quantitative. It was just this juxtaposition that was responsible for
the Woni group using a watch to time their performances, so that they
could more closely achieve the three-minute ideal they found on East
African popular recordings. They, like many other Kpelle people,
moved between the quantitative and the qualitative modes of time reckoning. They learned new ways of patterning their lives and their music.

CHAPTER 6

Surveying the Trip: Cutting the Edge

∝

The dancer and the drummer cut off the edge together.
—*Kpelle Musician*

You have traveled to places in the central Liberia region of Bong County, listened to the music, watched the dancers, experienced the excitement of a performance, and discovered how ideas about music learned from Kpelle performers reflect their life styles and values for daily living. You've used information from ethnomusicologists' research of performances in Liberia, other parts of West Africa, and the continent at large.

Your experience is not unlike the time I was also in Monrovia in 1976, waiting to go back to the United States after my doctoral dissertation fieldwork. I wrote to one of my advisors, Alan P. Merriam:

> We are in Monrovia making final preparations to leave in three days. It is wonderfully peaceful compared to our last days in Totota with people all stopping to say good-bye and bringing chickens, palm oil, and assorted produce for us to take back to the U.S. I think we both feel that all in all we had a wonderful year and were genuinely sad at having to leave some of the real friends we made. We have also become so accustomed to having so many people around us that I am sure it will be difficult to readjust to living relatively alone. (Stone 1976)

CENTRAL THEMES

It is now possible to distill all of the ideas into overarching themes that help to organize what one knows about Kpelle music, in particular, and West African music in general, based on the focus on Kpelle music in a particular time and place.

1. **Music links sounds to dance, instrument playing, and even speech in narration.** Thus, people experience a close linkage, moving easily from one medium to another. Music can hardly be thought of without including the other arts. To make a musical sound, one almost assumes a dance motion to accompany it. Words underlie rhythmic patterns. They all mesh quite closely. Within this alloy, the movement from indigenous to popular and religious music is very fluid, and the categories themselves are very porous. Aspects of music from other cultures blend into indigenous Kpelle performance as we saw most vividly in the music of the Woni group, which drew on Western as well as East African popular music.

2. **All people are expected to be minimally competent in music making, particularly singing and dancing.** Like learning to speak, young adults demonstrate their competence in dancing when they are initiated into adulthood through societies like the Poro or Sande. And all their lives they participate as members of choruses. Thus, the concept of an audience that gazes upon other people who are performing has little meaning in this area. Music moves people to participate in some fashion and all participants at an event are considered to be contributing to the event in a fairly active way.

The exceptionally talented performers receive special tutoring in playing instruments, singing, or dancing. Those who excel are believed to have the aid of a tutelary spirit, a powerful relationship that can be both rewarding and, occasionally, treacherous if not respected.

3. **The instruments played by the Kpelle are extensions of their human performers. Instruments and humans have voices.** Some instruments may have human attributes, including names and body parts. In special cases they may receive food sacrifices. But in all cases, they are much more than merely material objects or artifacts. Among the Kpelle, these instruments are divided into two categories: those that are struck and those that are blown.

4. **Performers in a broad range of musical events relate to one another in a part-counterpart arrangement.** That is, every soloist generally has a supporting soloist. These two performers are, in turn, balanced by the chorus. Instrumentalists have a parallel structure in which the master drummer, playing the goblet drum, is supported by the drummer playing the two-headed cylindrical drum.

This arrangement means that no single performer is overly prominent and even soloists are part of a complex, interdependent web of musicians and audience numbers. And the term given to "chorus" of "responding underneath people" nicely portrays that support.

5. **The most valued form of performance among the Kpelle is hocket, or the combining of facets, where each player or singer contributes a short pattern that interlocks with the motifs of other performers.** Bush clearing songs and horn ensemble music for chiefs are two important examples of hocketing.

This hocket performance, like the part-counterpart arrangement, underscores the emphasis in Kpelle performance upon complex interaction that emphasizes individuality of parts within a larger unity.

6. **Performers value the faceting of sound into small components that are then recombined. This faceting appears in singing, dancing, and song text alike.** Parallels exist in textiles, masks, and other visual arts where the surface is broken into multiple units and, in the case of masks, a variety of planes. Facets, whether created of melodic and rhythmic patterns or cloth designs or surfaces of wood appear to be a fundamental aesthetic value that permeate the arts whether they are visual or performing in nature.

7. **Tone color or timbre is much noticed and admired in music.** Musicians love a variety of tone colors and add rattles to all manner of instruments to enhance the array of tone colors. A kind of pungent buzzing is considered delightful. Sounds that we might find nonmusical are layered onto the sustained pitches for added color. Within the texts, words often portray and delineate timbre with onomatopoeic sound. Color in the visual realm, like that of sound, is bold, admired, and noticed. Disparate colors in sound and cloth are juxtaposed and valued.

8. **Musicians create rhythms that are often asymmetrical and then interlock with other performers in a very precise way.** These layered polyrhythms are often communicated with mnemonic syllables that describe both rhythmic and timbral qualities.

9. **Key soloists are expected to improvise against the background of a rich and layered backdrop.** Each performance demonstrates that the essence of creativity is to spontaneously compose in rich variation onto a backdrop of complex repetition.

10. **Continuity in music performance builds through the density of many discrete parts.** One is not necessarily causal or linear to another. The epic doesn't build from birth of the hero onward, but proceeds in a variety of order depending upon the situation.

11. **Parallels to these central themes abound in everyday Kpelle life, and reinforce our conviction that these themes have some importance for the Kpelle conceptualization.** So whether one is singing in a tight hocket or greeting someone in a close-paced back and forth of pleasantries, faceting of sound is paramount.

Performance in West Africa, as illustrated by that of the Kpelle musicians, is built on multilayers of richly varied rhythms and timbres. The layers of sound and text in musical performance show fertile imaginations that comment upon everyday life as well as build ideas in special realms removed from the everyday sphere of reality.

Glossary

∞

Fee a category of instruments that are blown; one of two major categories of instruments for the Kpelle.

Fêli a goblet-shaped drum played with the hands by the master drummer.

Gbong-kpala a musical bow that is struck with a stick and resonated with the encircled mouth.

Gbung-gbung a two-headed cylindrical drum that is played with sticks and supports the goblet-shaped drum.

Hemiola ratio of 2 to 3; musically, the substitution of 3 beats for 2 or 2 beats for 3.

Kenemâ dance step that always ends a dance sequence and usually includes a cut-off cue.

Koli-gong-song-pele a musical event that centers on a character who performs witchcraft that was developed in 1975–76 in the Gbeyilataa area.

Konîng triangular frame-zither with a gourd resonator and rattles.

Kono hand-held slit drums played by bush-clearing ensembles.

Kora harp-lute found in West Africa and played by praise singers.

Kutindingo a conical drum played with one stick and one hand by the Mandinka people in The Gambia.

Kuu work cooperative that people form in order to clear the bush for making a rice farm or for planting the rice.

Lôking dance step that emphasizes a forward movement by quickly stepping first right with the right foot and then left with the left foot.

Meni-pele   chante-fable; dramatized folktale that is accompanied by instruments and a choral background.

Mnemonic   syllables that serve as memory aids and indicate pitch, rhythm, and timbre of musical phrases.

Muu   short repeating pattern sung by a part of the chorus to enhance the sound.

Muu-siye-belai   Owl-raising-people. Singers who embellish the performance with added ostinato patterns as the improvising becomes more and more elaborate.

Nga-tee   "cutting off the edge"; a cue that is executed in dance or song and indicates the end of a phase of a musical event.

Nyéng-nyéng   rattles, often added to an instrument, made of seed pods, Coke bottle caps, or other metal.

Owl-raising-people   "Muu-siye-belai" or singers who embellish the performance with added ostinato patterns as the improvising becomes more and more elaborate.

Pêle   musical event, children's play, game.

Polyrhythm   simultaneous use of different rhythms.

Poro   generic West African term for men's secret society to which all men belong. In Kpelle specifically, *polong*.

Sande   generic West African term for women's secret society to which all women belong. In Kpelle specifically, *saning*.

Sokokpâ   dance step that involves turning first one direction and then the other.

Song catcher   supporting singer who is referred to as the *tomo-song-nûu*.

Timeline   any of several repeating patterns underlying much African music and usually played by a high-pitched struck idiophone.

Tomo   repeating ostinato pattern sung between solo lines.

Tomo-song-nûu   supporting singer who is sometimes referred to as the song catcher or the *tomo* catcher because he or she fills in after the soloists before the chorus enters.

TUBS   Time Unit Box System of notation developed in 1962 for teaching African rhythm.

Turu transverse horn of wood or ivory or animal horn that is played by royal musicians.

Woi-meni-pele epic that tells of the life and adventures of the hero Woi; includes instrumental accompaniment and choral background.

Yale a category of instruments that are struck, including plucked stringed instruments, drums, and rattles. One of two major categories of instruments that the Kpelle people designate.

References

∞

Armstrong, Robert Plant. 1971. *The Affecting Presence*. Urbana: Unversity of Illinois Press.

Battuta, Ibn. 1858. *Voyages d'Ibn Batoutah*. Translated by C. Defrémery and B. R. Sanguinetti. Paris: Imprimerie Nationale.

Becker, Alton L. 1979. "Text Building, Epistemology, and Aesthetics in Javanese Shadow Theatre," In *The Imagination of Reality: Essays in Southeast Asian Coherence Systems*, edited by A. L. Becker and Aram A. Yengoyan, 211–43. Norwood, N.J.: Ablex.

Berliner, Paul. 1978. *The Soul of Mbira*. Berkeley: University of California Press.

Blacking, John. 1969. *Process and Product in Human Society*. Johannesburg: Witwatersrand University Press.

Bohannan, Paul. 1953. "Concepts of Time among the Tiv of Nigeria." *Southwestern Journal of Anthropology* 9(3):251–62.

Bordieu, Pierre. 1963. "The Attitude of the Algerian Peasant Toward Time." In *Mediterranean Countrymen*, edited by J. Pitt-Rivers, 52–72. The Hague: Mouton.

Boyd, Alan. 1977. "The Dimension of Time in the Definition of the Situation with Reference to *Maludi*." Unpublished manuscript.

Brown, Joe. 1994. "Djimo Kouyate." *Washington Post*, 28 January.

Charry, Eric. 2000. *Mande Music*. Chicago: University of Chicago Press.

Chernoff, John Miller. 1979. *African Rhythm and African Sensibility*. Chicago: University of Chicago Press.

Euba, Akin. 1992. "Creating Authentic Forms of New African Art Music." International Conference on African Music and Dance: Problems and Prospects. Working Documents. Bellagio Study and Conference Center, Bellagio, Italy, 12–16 October.

Gibson, Gloria J. and Daniel B. Reed. 2002. *Music and Culture of West Africa: The Strauss Expedition*. Bloomington: Indiana University Press. 2 CD-ROMs.

Herzog, George. 1930. Liberia, Dimiah, Djabo. Sound recordings, 236 cylinders, documentation. Deposited at the Indiana University, Archives of Traditional Music, Accession No. 54-223-F.

Himes, Geoffrey. 1995. "Maal's African Dance Mix." *Washington Post*, 20 January.

King, Anthony. 1960. "Employments of the 'Standard Pattern' in Yoruba Music." *African Music* 2(3):51–54.

Knight, Roderic. 1974. "Mandinka Drumming." *African Arts* 7:25–35.

Koetting, James. 1970. "Analysis and Notation of West African Drum Ensemble Music." *Selected Reports, Institute of Ethnomusicology, UCLA* 1(3):115–46

Kubik, Gerhard. 1965. "Transcription of Mangwilo Xylophone Music from Film Strips." *African Music* 3(4):35–51.

———. 1983. "The Emics of African Musical Rhythm." Unpublished manuscript.

Maal, Baaba. 1994. *Firin in Fouta*. Mango [Records]. Compact disc.

McNaughton, Patrick, John H. Hanson, dele jegede, Ruth M. Stone, and N. Brian Winchester. 2000. *Five Windows into Africa*. CD-ROM. Bloomington: Indiana University Press.

Nenei-kole, Feme. 2003. Letter to Ruth M. Stone, August 23.

Nketia, J. H. Kwabena. 1958. "Traditional Music of the Ga People." *African Music* 2(1):21–27.

O'Meara, Patrick and Phyllis Martin. 1995. *Africa*. Third Edition. Bloomington: Indiana University Press.

Stone, Ruth M. 1972. "Meni-Pele: A Musical Dramatic Folktale of the Kpelle." *Liberian Studies Journal* 4: 31–46.

———. 1975. Fieldwork Journal. Unpublished.

———. 1976. Letter to Alan P. Merriam. 8 November 1976.

———. 1982. *Let the Inside Be Sweet*. Bloomington: Indiana University Press.

———. 1988. *Dried Millet Breaking*. Bloomington: Indiana University Press.

———. 1998. *The Garland Encyclopedia of World Music: Africa*. New York: Garland Publishing.

Stone, Ruth M. and Verlon L. 1970. Liberia, Bong County, Kpelle. Sound recordings, 24 sound tape reels: analog, documentation. Deposited at the Indiana University Archives of Traditional Music, Accession No. 73-052-F.

———. 1975. Liberia, Bong County, Kpelle. Sound recordings, 72 sound tape reels: analog, documentation. Deposited at the Indiana University Archives of Traditional Music, Accession No. 82-434-F.

———. 1981. "Event, Feedback and Analysis: Research Media in the Study of Music Events." *Ethnomusicology* 25:215–25.

Thompson, Robert Ferris. 1974. *African Art in Motion: Icon and Act*. Los Angeles: University of California Press.

Whitehurst, D. W. "Whitehurst Journal." *African Repository and Colonial Journal* 12(1836):105–315.

Resources

∞

As you continue on this journey, you may want to explore some other resources that will provide you with more knowledge about Africa. To get a general introduction to the continent, consult *Africa* (O'Meara and Martin 1995) to understand more about social formations, political issues, and the arts. A supplement to *Africa* is the CD-ROM *Five Windows into Africa* (McNaughton, Hanson, jegede, Stone, and Winchester 2000), which provides a more interactive introduction to the continent. There you can explore a Kpelle funeral event, which I studied in detail, and view a twenty-minute excerpt of a videotape, which documents the two days of performance. For a general introduction to music of the African continent, examine *Africa: Garland Encyclopedia of World Music* (Stone 1998). The annotated list of resources provides additional supplementary material for moving beyond this work.

Africa

Gray, John. 1991. *African Music: A Bibliographical Guide to the Traditional, Popular, Arts and Liturgical Musics of Sub-Saharan Africa.*. New York and Westport, Ct.: Greenwood.

O'Meara, Patrick and Phyllis Martin (eds.). 1995. *Africa*. Third Edition. Bloomington: Indiana University Press. An introductory text that examines various aspects of culture in Africa. The authors of *Five Windows* also have articles in this introductory text that supplement the CD-ROM on Africa.

Stone, Ruth M. (ed.). 1999. *Handbook in African Music*. New York: Routledge. Survey articles on music in Africa, including the examination of the guitar in Africa, popular music in Nigeria, and an examination of time in Kpelle music making.

McNaughton, Patrick, John Hanson, dele jegede, Ruth M. Stone, and Brian Winchester. 2000. *Five Windows into Africa*. CD-ROM. Bloomington: Indiana University Press. The five "windows" provide interactive audiovisual glimpses at a funeral event in Liberia, popular music in Lagos,

Nigeria, chimurenga music in Zimbabwe, masked performance in Mali, and Islamic performance of prayers in Ghana.

West Africa

Adzenyah, Abraham Kobena, Dumisani Maraire, and Judith Cook Tucker. 1997 [1987]. *Let Your Voice Be Heard! Songs from Ghana and Zimbabwe*. Danbury, Connecticut : World Music Press. This collection of Ghanaian and Zimbabwean songs includes nineteen game songs from the vocal traditional of the Akan people of Ghana and the Shona of Zimbabwe. The work includes musical transcriptions, lyrics with translation and a compact disc or cassette tape. There is also contextual information on the history and geography of the area represented by the music as well pedagogical information on creating the sound.

Charry, Eric. 2000. *Mande Music*. Chicago: University of Chicago Press. A comprehensive source on music of the Maninka across West Africa, including extensive discography.

Gibson, Gloria J. and Daniel B. Reed. 2002. *Music and Culture of West Africa*. Bloomington: Indiana University Press. 2 CD-ROM set. This project traces the historical expedition of Laura Boulton in Mali during the 1930s as she recorded instruments indigenous to the region. Silent film footage and audio recordings from the expedition are supplemented with more contemporary recordings of music in West Africa that illustrate the sounds of the various instruments. There are several excellent interactive exercises that allow students to compose in hocket in the style of West African transverse horns and to experiment with drum patterns of a drum ensemble.

Hale, Thomas 1998. *Griots and Griottes*. Bloomington: Indiana University Press. A comprehensive discussion of epic singers in West Africa, beginning with early historical accounts.

Knight, Roderic. 1972. *Jali Nyam Suso: Kora Player of The Gambia*. Oberlin, OH: Roderic Knight, 89 Pyle Road, Oberlin, OH 44074. Videotape, 20 minutes. This film was made at the University of Washington at the end of a one-year residency by Jali Nyama Suso, a renowned player and teacher of the 21-string Mandinka harp-lute, the kora. The performances are exemplary of Nyama Suso's energetic style. An 8-page booklet provides background information and a synopsis of the song contents.

———. 1970–82. *Music of the Mande*, Oberlin, OH: Roderic Knight, 89 Pyle Road, Oberlin, OH 44074. Videotape, 62 minutes. This film was made in The Gambia in 1970 and 1982 and is of historic value. A 24-page booklet contains technical notes and contextual information.

Locke, David. 1998 [1987]. *Drum Gahu: The Rhythms of West African Drumming*. Incline Village, NV: White Cliffs Media. Audio cassettes also available. Provides systematic analysis and instruction for a selected dance performance from the Ewe people of Ghana.

Locke, David and Godwin Agbeli. 1992. *Kpegisu: A War Drum of the Ewe.* Incline Village, NV: White Cliffs Media. Videocassette, 30 minutes. (Accompanying book available.) A videorecording of Ewe performance film in Ghana with footage selected from a day long ritual performance.

Mali Lolo! Stars of Mali. 2003. Washington, D. C.: Smithsonian Folkways Recordings, SFW 40508. Features the Super Rail Band, Grammy-winner Ali Farka Touré, *kora* masters Toumani Diabaté and Ballaké Sissoko, Wassoulou diva Oumou Sangaré, guitarist and singer Habib Koité and his Bamada group and more of Mali's best talent.

Reed, Daniel B. 2003. *Dan Ge Performance.* Bloomington: Indiana University Press. This book explores Ge masked performance in Côte d'Ivoire in terms of music and ritual relationships, identity issues, and incorporation of global performance practices.

Toepke, Alvaro and Angel Serrno. 1998. *The Language You Cry In.* San Francisco: California Newsreel. 52 minute video. English with Mende and English subtitles. The film traces the history of a burial song of the Mende people as slaves brought it to the southern coast of the United States. A Gullah family from the United States travels to Sierra Leone to meet with villagers where the song is remembered. Issues of memory, archival documentation, and connections between Africans and African Americans are explored.

Liberia—Kpelle

Stone, Ruth M. 1982. *Let the Inside Be Sweet.* Bloomington: Indiana University Press. This work is an introductory ethnography to the music of the Kpelle, particularly focusing on their interpretations of terms and practices.

———. 1986. "African Music Performed." In *Africa*, edited by Patrick O'Meara and Phyllis Martin. Bloomington: Indiana University Press, pp. 233–48. Revised Edition. An introduction to the music of Africa, this article illustrates examples from the author's fieldwork among the Kpelle of Liberia, West Africa.

———. 1988. *Dried Millet Breaking.* Bloomington: Indiana University Press. This work examines the temporal dimension of the Woi epic among the Kpelle of Liberia, considering how text and music interact to create various aspects of time.

———. 2000. "Traveling Home: Music, Politics, and the Commemoration of a Life." In *Five Windows on Africa.* Bloomington: Indiana University Press. This interactive CD-ROM provides one twenty-minute videotaped segment of a funeral event in Liberia, West Africa. The analysis examines the funeral as performance, politics, aesthetics, and other aspects of culture interaction in the context of music making. Includes examples of the present author's field notes as well as audio examples of instruments, interviews with performers, and other musical illustrations.

Stone, Ruth M. and Verlon L. 1972. *Music of the Kpelle of Liberia*. Sound recording, FE 4385. New York: Ethnic Folkways. (Available through Smithsonian Folkways) This recording surveys a range of music recorded in the central Liberian area in 1970 in Bong County. Instrumental examples include the triangular frame-zither, slit drum, transverse horn ensemble, mouth bow, and double-headed hourglass drum.

Index

∞